The old-time pamphlet ethos is back, with some of the most challenging work being done today. Prickly Paradigm Press is devoted to giving serious authors free rein to say what's right and what's wrong about their disciplines and about the world, including what's never been said before. The result is intellectuals unbound, writing unconstrained and creative texts about meaningful matters.

"Long live Prickly Paradigm Press.... Long may its flaming pamphlets lift us from our complacency."
—Ian Hacking

Prickly Paradigm is marketed and distributed by
The University of Chicago Press.

www.press.uchicago.edu

A list of current and future titles can be found on our website and at the back of this pamphlet.

www.prickly-paradigm.com

Executive Publisher
Marshall Sahlins

Publishers
Peter Sahlins
Ramona Naddaff
Bernard Sahlins
Seminary Co-op Bookstore

Editor
Matthew Engelke
info@prickly-paradigm.com

David Hahn, Editorial Assistant
Design and layout by Bellwether Manufacturing.

The Ecology of Others

The Ecology of Others

Philippe Descola

Translated from the French
by Geneviève Godbout and Benjamin P. Luley

PRICKLY PARADIGM PRESS
CHICAGO

Prickly Paradigm Press, LLC
5629 South University Avenue
Chicago, Il 60637

www.prickly-paradigm.com

ISBN: 9780984201020
LCCN: 2012948394

Printed in the United States of America on acid-free paper.

Contents

Foreword to the English edition

The main portion of the present essay was initially written for a lecture delivered in Paris in 2007 at the invitation of the French Institute for Agronomic Research (INRA), as part of a program aimed at fostering epistemological and sociological reflexivity among the scientists of this institution, the largest in Europe in its domain. The lecture was thus intended for an audience mainly composed of biologists, agronomists, chemists, earth scientists and other researchers in the natural sciences, who were concerned with the social issues raised by their work but had little knowledge of how the social sciences dealt with these questions. One of the reasons for my invitation to speak was a book I had published in French not long before (in English, *Beyond Nature and Culture*, The University of Chicago Press, in press) in which I developed a general model accounting for the diversity of relations between humans and non-humans. Rather than summing up the contents of the book, however, I chose to discuss what I have come to call the anthropology of nature. The argument combined a critical appraisal of the anthropological approaches of the relations between societies and their environments with a clarification of the epistemological foundations of my own perspective on that question.

The lecture was thus not intended for anthropologists. This is why I did not hesitate to enter into particulars, knowing that my audience was mainly unaware of the intricacies of the anthropological and philosophical debates about the place of Humankind in Nature, especially among English-speaking scholars. Thus, I was not a little surprised when Marshall Sahlins told me that the booklet resulting from the lecture would fit well in the Prickly Paradigm series. He assured me that an anglophone audience could also find an interest in heated debates about the role of nature in shaping human destiny, some of these debates being almost forgotten yet still relevant, others much fresher although still confined to the enjoyment of a happy few. Let the reader be judge of whether he was right.

To Raphaël Larrère, who invited me to give the lecture at INRA, to Marshall Sahlins, who, perhaps ill-advisedly, asked me to publish it in English, to Anne-Christine Taylor, who helped me revise the translation and to Matthew Engelke, the editor, go my warmest thanks.

Philippe Descola
Le Coy, August 2012

Introduction

During the second half of the nineteenth century the respective approaches and domains of the sciences of nature and of the sciences of culture were finally delineated. They were so in theory, through the development of epistemological works that emphasized the methodological differences between the two fields of study, and they were so in practice, through the final establishment of the compartmentalized organization of universities and research institutes with which we are familiar today. As with all specialization processes, this partitioning of competences has had some positive effects, inasmuch as the concentration of shared know-how, habits of thoughts, qualification systems, means of work and evaluation mechanisms within given learned communities has multiplied the conditions for the production of knowledge. However, the reinforced institutional division between the sciences and the humanities has also had the consequence of making much more difficult the comprehension of situations in which material phenomena and moral phenomena are combined. The sciences that had chosen as their object of study the relationship between the physical dimensions and the cultural dimensions of human activities—geography, psychology, or ethology, for example—ultimately found themselves divided from within between the partisans of one approach or the other, each finally deciding upon a divorce, amicable in the best cases.

Anthropology has not escaped this kind of partitioning, and it is essentially this issue that the present pamphlet will engage. A first split occurred as early as the late-nineteenth century between the approach to human diversity through biological traits and the approach through cultural traits, so that the initial ambition to grasp the unity of Humankind in the diversity of its expressions eventually disappeared: physical anthropology inherited the goal of establishing unity beyond variations, while social anthropology contented itself, most of the time, with accounting for variations against the background of a taken for granted unity. Recent attempts to rekindle the dialogue, as exemplified by the development of human sociobiology, evolutionary psychology, or memetics, have not yielded any convincing results so far, either because their treatment of cultural facts is of such weakness that it erases their particularisms, or because the biological mechanisms invoked as the origin of a given social fact are so general that they lose their explanatory power.

Human sociobiology devotes itself to examining the effects on institutions of the practices that maximize reproductive advantages, while evolutionary psychology attempts to recover within contemporary human aptitudes the behaviors that were formerly selected during the course of phylogenesis for the adaptive advantage they procured. In both cases, there is such an abyss between the simplicity of the mechanism invoked and the complexity of the institution that originated from it that it becomes impossible to assign to this mechanism a causal action over the great variety of forms that the institution assumes. Kinship is the classical example of this shortcoming. From the point of view of sociobiology, the function of kinship ties is to codify and stabilize altruism, that is to say one's disposition to protect relatives at the peril of one's life to ensure the survival through them of a part of one's genetic heritage. But this circular reasoning hardly allows for an explanation of the great diversity in the means of classifying and treating kin related individuals, means of which many have precisely for consequence either to exclude from the circle of close kinsmen blood-relatives with whom the rate of genetic similarity is nevertheless high; or, to the contrary, to include individuals with whom no genetic relation exists. In regard to memetics, a term coined by Richard Dawkins, the concept aims to supersede the current sciences of culture by putting forward an approach founded on the study of the natural selection of "memes," or elements of information which constitute culture and which, in some cases, may provide an adaptive advantage. This theory reaches its critical point when it finds itself in the impossible position of providing a non-trivial definition of what might constitute a discrete unit of information within a cultural system, a classical problem in anthropology ever since the debates of the end of the nineteenth century concerning the diffusion of techniques and ideas that the "memeticians" seem to ignore completely.

However, the division in ways of approaching the diversity of human institutions does not lie solely between physical anthropology and its neo-Darwinian revivals on the one hand, and the diverse sectors of social and cultural anthropology on the other. The divide also runs through the latter, perhaps even more clearly than in any other discipline that studies interfacial objects. Indeed, for more than a century social and cultural anthropology has defined itself as the science of the mediations between nature and culture, between the physical determinations that condition the life of humans, including their organism, and the dizzying diversity of meanings with which these determinations are vested. The duality of the world, its separation between universal material regularities and particular systems of value, has become the constitutive dimension of the object of anthropology, the challenge it has attempted to take on by deploying a wealth of ingenuity in order to reduce the gap between the two planes of reality.

Yet, and this is what I would like to demonstrate in this pamphlet, such a task remains impossible to carry out so long as we continue to accept the initial premise, namely the fact that human experience must be understood as resulting from the coexistence of two fields of phenomena governed by distinct principles. The study of a controversy will serve as an opening for this discussion; academic polemics have the advantage of presenting antagonistic positions in a more clear-cut way than is usual. The controversy at hand opposes, on one side, those who posit that the relationship of humans to their environments must be considered in terms of the constraints induced by the use, control and transformation of so-called natural resources; and on the other side those who, instead, approach this relationship by way of the particularities of the symbolic treatment of a nature that is nevertheless reputed to be homogeneous in its limits and its mode of functioning. As sharp as it might appear, the conflict between the two positions nevertheless does not really call into question the presuppositions that they share concerning the duality of nature and society. It will therefore be necessary to expose these presuppositions by exploring the ways in which they affect the various stages of the anthropological approach: the definition of its object of study, the methods employed to deal with it, the debates regarding the status of knowledge about nature and, notably, the difficulty of accounting for the manner in which this last question presents itself to the Moderns while using the habitual tools developed for the ethnological study of the non-moderns.

Lastly, we will ask ourselves how to avoid these difficulties. How to recompose nature and society, humans and non-humans, individuals and collectives, in a new assemblage in which they would no longer present themselves as distributed between substances, processes, and representations, but as the instituted expression of relationships between multiple entities whose ontological status and capacity for action vary according to the positions they occupy in relation to one another? An ecology of relationships borrowing from different behavioral and life sciences is fostered by this recomposition, of which one can here and there discern the premises and to which anthropology will be able to contribute only by agreeing to give up a great part of its anthropocentrism.

1
The Clam Debate

The sociology and the anthropology of sciences have taught us that a good way to understand the status of a scientific problem is to study controversies. The one I have chosen as an opening is somewhat dated, but it synthesizes well the inextricable difficulties anthropology has taken on when it first constituted itself, around the end of the nineteenth century, as a science of interface between nature and culture. The polemic in question developed in 1976 in the anthropological journal *L'Homme*. It opposed, on either side of the Atlantic, two great figures of the discipline: Claude Lévi-Strauss, founder of structural anthropology, and Marvin Harris, then professor at Columbia University and mastermind of cultural materialism. The debate—and it was a heated one—did not concern an Australian kinship system or a ritual of New Guinea, but the dimension, color and dietary value of the siphons of the clam, that large bivalve so common along the coasts of North America.

On the proper use of siphons

Let us briefly recall the circumstances of the controversy. Four years earlier, Lévi-Strauss had delivered the
Gildersleeve Lecture at Barnard College in which he
specified his conception of the respective role of the
operations of the mind and of ecological determinants
in the work carried out by mythic thought when it
organizes elements of the natural environment into
meaningful systems. For him, it was a matter of
responding—in the very place in which they arose—to
the accusations of idealism leveled against him by a
growing number of North-American anthropologists
who saw in the constraints exerted on a society by its
environment, and in the adaptive responses those
constraints provoked, the origin and the cause of most
cultural specificities. Reiterating in his lecture an argument already laid out in *The Savage Mind*, Lévi-Strauss
endeavored to demonstrate that there was nothing
automatic or predictable in the way in which a society
selects one aspect or another from its habitat to endow
it with a particular signification and integrate it to
mythic constructions. Because neighboring cultures
often identify completely different salient features in a
same animal or in a same plant, they can also give an
identical symbolic function to species belonging to a
different genus, or even a different kingdom. The arbitrariness that governs the choice of distinctive traits
imputed to a component of local ecosystems is nevertheless moderated by the fact that these traits are organized into coherent systems, which can in turn be
analyzed as transformations of one another according
to a small number of rules. In short, while the myths

originating from nearby tribes might use entirely distinct properties of fauna and flora to the same end, the structure of those myths is not random, and it organizes itself according to the mirror-like effects of inversion and symmetry.

To illustrate these basic principles of structural anthropology, Lévi-Strauss had undertaken in his lecture to analyze some myths from North America. Those upon which the controversy turned came from British Columbia and were collected by Franz Boas. The Bella Bella, a coastal tribe, recount that a child captured by an ogress succeeded, after diverse adventures, in recovering his freedom thanks to the advice of a protector spirit. The father of the child was then able to recuperate all of the ogress' belongings—copper plates, furs, tanned hides, dried meat...—which he distributed to his fellow tribesmen, thus providing the origin of the potlatch. The manner by which the child rid himself of his captor is unusual: having taken the siphons of some clams the ogress had gathered, he placed them over the tips of his fingers and waved them in front of the ogress, provoking in her such a fright that she fell down a cliff and killed herself. Why, then, asks Lévi-Strauss, would a giant and a cannibal be terrorized by these insignificant little tubes, in fact so depreciated that they are reputed not to be edible?

According to Lévi-Strauss, the answer to this puzzle can be found in a myth of the Chilcotin, a tribe not far from the Bella Bella but living inland, beyond the mountain range that borders a great part of the Pacific Coast of Canada. This myth tells the story of a boy raised by Owl, a powerful sorcerer, who treated him well. After several years, the parents of the boy discovered his place of hiding and convinced him to return with them. Owl having given chase to them, the young hero scared him off by brandishing like claws his hands which he had fitted with the horns of mountain goats. Resourceful as he was, the boy also took care to seize all of Owl's *Dentaliidae* shells, those small white shells which from then on constituted the most precious good of the Chilcotin. One can easily see, Lévi-Strauss comments, that the Bella Bella myth and the Chilcotin myth have the same narrative framework since they both recount the story of a child using artificial claws to rid himself of his captor and to get hold of a treasure. Yet while the stratagems employed and the objectives pursued are identical, the means of the former and the nature of the latter are symmetrically reversed: the siphons of the clams, soft and inoffensive objects coming from the marine world, make it possible to obtain the terrestrial treasures of the ogress, while the mountain goat horns, hard and dangerous objects coming from the terrestrial world, make it possible to obtain the marine resources of Owl. According to Lévi-Strauss, this inversion can be explained as much by the rules of transformation specific to the logic of myths as by the ecological and techno-economical materials that fuel it. Indeed, in coastal tribes the products of the sea are part of daily life while products of which the ogress disposes are obtained through exchange with tribes of the interior, who in turn procure through this channel the *Dentaliidae* they so desire. The flow of objects is thus analogous to the chiasm that characterizes the mythical transformation: the appendix of a mollusk, devalued by one group because it is common, maintains with the shell of another mollusk, valued by the others because of its rarity, the same reversed symmetrical relationship which prevails between the respective natural environments of the two types of population.

Such an interpretation could not receive the approval of Harris, in the eyes of whom the majority of myths, rituals, or dietary behaviors can be reduced to a practical utility and are better explained by the adaptive function they fulfill than by a game of abstruse mental operations. Feeling keenly the sting of the Gildersleeve Lecture delivered in his absence, at an institution dependent upon the university where he was teaching, Harris went on to reproach Lévi-Strauss, and in very incisive terms, for having ignored that the modest clams of the ogress were in fact horse clams (*Tresus capax* Gould), very large bivalves whose siphon can shoot water up a meter high; that far from being a depreciated food, this siphon is a choice morsel packed with proteins; that it is adorned with a claw-like appendage; that it contains an especially toxic micro-organism whose harmful effects have drawn the attention of the CIA; and lastly that it obviously resembles a penis, the term by which the Bella Bella refer to it. In other words, our ogress was not frightened by soft and inoffensive little tubes, but by ten enormous, horned and poisonous phalluses that the child brandished under her nose. Hence, it is not useful to mobilize the Chilcotin myth to explain the Bella Bella myth, nor to invoke complex chiasms moreover unsupported, according to Harris, by the ethnography of the region.

To this critique, and its "rampant empiricism," Lévi-Strauss responded by a one-upmanship of conchological and ethnographic erudition. Suffice it to mention here the main point of Lévi-Strauss demonstration: everything in the myth indicates that the bivalves in question were not horse clams but indeed ordinary clams or even, in certain versions of the myth, unspecified shells. An Owikeno version of the myth of the ogress even replaces the siphons by the byssi, the bundles of filaments by which mussels attach to rocks. It is thus futile to force a correspondence between a given mythic signification and the specific properties of a particular organ of a single kind of mollusk. The content of myths is not fixed for all eternity, and the latter play upon a range where, as in the present case, diverse empirical illustrations of a same organ are spread out, as are those of different organs which can belong to distinct animal families. Structural analysis demonstrates that all the elements of this paradigm are usable by mythic thought "so long, at the price of the transformations that it is incumbent upon us to reconstruct, as they allow for the expression of meanings of the same type not individually, but in opposition to other terms that vary at the same time as them."

The quarrel of the clams was closed, but the underlying problem remained. Should one consider culture as an adaptive system responding to natural constraints and thus ultimately explainable by mechanisms subject to the laws of matter and of life; or should one see in culture a distinct order of reality which only sustains relationships of a contingent type with the ecological world and the necessities of human metabolism? In other words, are the sciences of culture autonomous, or can they only achieve rigorousness by borrowing part of their methods and some of their results from the natural sciences? One can here recognize a question that late-nineteenth century epistemology believed to have settled, but that anthropology continues, over a century later to ask with the same urgency. To better understand the reasons for this permanence, we must return for a moment to the theoretical position championed by Lévi-Strauss' opponent.

Conjectural ecology

Marvin Harris is the somewhat heterodox heir to a materialist current of North-American anthropology which had formed in the 1950s around Julian Steward, the inventor of "cultural ecology." Steward's ambition was to introduce geographical causality to the analysis of social realities, as a means of scientifically grounding the comparative method, thus taking up a project previously illustrated by Clark Wissler and Alfred Kroeber when they attempted to establish a correlation between the cultural areas of Native North Americans and the ecological zones of the continent. However, in contrast to these two authors, still marked by the influence of German diffusionism, Steward located his enterprise within a clearly evolutionist perspective. This involved isolating the constants in the morphology and social functions of populations belonging to different cultural areas but subjected to similar environmental conditions, and then explaining the changes these societies underwent as a consequence of the successive reorganizations of their mode of adaptation to the environment under the influence of various pressures. According to Steward, ecological constraints act most visibly upon the "cultural core," an assemblage of techniques, behaviors and institutions linked to the exploitation of natural resources. The heart of a society and its dynamic framework are thus constituted by these sectors of social, political, and religious systems which can be shown to intervene in a direct manner in the management of the environment: distribution of dwellings, division of labor, functions of authority, modes of transmitting rights over resources, ceremonies associated with the production of subsistence, etc. Because of the homology postulated between different cultural cores, societies seemingly quite different from one another might from then on be grouped by types—patrilineal bands, tribes, or chiefdoms, for example—each representing a stage of the multilinear evolution.

Such an explanation, however, lets a number of distinctive elements of a society pass through its net—aesthetics, moral values, mythology, certain religious beliefs or ritual attitudes, for example. These elements appear disconnected from the means of adaptation to environmental constraints, and would thus be amenable to a non-deterministic interpretation. For Steward, these "secondary traits" depend on the vagaries of cultural borrowing or local innovation, and it is because their contents and modes of expression are so diverse, and their particularisms so sharply highlighted by those who adhere to them as symbols of their collective identity, that all these differences in style and in value come to occlude the profound structural analogies that exist between societies exploiting comparable ecosystems with a similar techno-economic core. Here lies the ambiguity of Steward's approach—notable in his synthesis on South-American cultural areas—which combines an evolutionist and deterministic perspective in the comparative analysis of the mechanisms of sociocultural adaptation to the environment, with a diffusionist and relativist point of view when accounting for the more immaterial aspects of culture.

Some among the researchers who claim the intellectual heritage of Steward have pursued the same line of inquiry. Archaeologists for the most part, they sought to find the causes for diachronic variations in sociocultural evolution through the study of systems of interaction between a given habitat and techniques. Their method is simple, even simplistic: it involves isolating a limiting ecological factor—the differential fertility of soils, for example—which should shed light on the variations in the degree of institutional complexity achieved by the societies subjected to this constraint. Others, by contrast, with Harris as a foremost leader, have attempted to eliminate the epistemological and methodological difficulty from which Steward had been unable to escape, namely the recourse to two very different types of explanations for different parts of society: determinist and evolutionist for that which pertains to the social use of resources, diffusionist and contingent for that which pertain to religion and values. And they did so by following the path already blazed, but imperfectly followed, by Steward; that is, they attempted to integrate the "secondary traits" to the finally unified field of ecological determinism. Bizarre superstitions, customs without an apparent function, the sweeping movements of religious imaginary, which had previously stumped the founder of cultural ecology, all became transparent. For the most audacious successors of Steward, ritualistic cannibalism, dietary prohibitions, medieval sorcery or messianic movements were but adaptive responses to the constraints of a given environment. In setting out to solve what Harris has called "the riddles of culture," ecological determinism, henceforth renamed "cultural materialism," could take over the totality of the social field thanks to a single method of explanation.

Thus annexed, the social field became however singularly restrained in its autonomy, reduced to a simple epiphenomenon of the mechanisms and processes that were a matter of biological causality. An appropriate illustration of such reductionism is the explanation of the dietary taboo on sloths among the Jivaro Indians put forward by Eric Ross in his 1978 article "Food Taboos, Diet and Hunting Strategy." A disciple of Harris, this author begins with the hypothesis that the prohibition against the consumption of tapir and *Cervidae* common to numerous Amerindian groups of the Amazon is the translation in a cultural principle of an unconscious optimization of work allocation: in terms of the ratio between the energy spent and the energy obtained, hunting big mammals, which are usually rare and shy, is allegedly more costly than pursuing small game, which is relatively abundant and easy to shoot. This strange calculation of optimization is inspired by a theory of rational decision-making derived from neoclassical economic doctrines, but which elides deliberate action on the part of the actor since a taboo is necessary to render it operational. This is no doubt because the Jivaro have yet to achieve the perfect intelligibility of means and ends specific to the modern *Homo oeconomicus*, and they thus need the nudge of a mysterious collective unconscious in order to make their subsistence techniques more efficient.

Such clear-sightedness on the part of culture also tolerates some exceptions since, not satisfied with abstaining solely from tapir and deer meat, the Jivaro also proscribe the consumption of mammals that are smaller and less rare, such as the sloth. And since utilitarian thought abhors useless institutions, it becomes necessary to explain the adaptive function fulfilled by this dietary taboo that no economic rationale would seem to justify. This explanation builds on the idea that sloths eat certain plants that are overlooked by other species of mammals, and that they would consequently be the only ones capable of converting this specific portion of the vegetal biomass into animal biomass (hence the necessity to preserve them). Moreover, their excrements ensure soil fertilization and thus favor the growth of certain species of trees, whose fruits are eaten precisely by several species of monkeys hunted by the Jivaro. According to Ross, those peaceful toothless creatures play an absolutely fundamental role in the trophic chain that goes from a group of vegetal species only usable by them to an animal population that constitutes an important source of protein for humans. It is that role that the wise and farsighted taboo is meant to perpetuate.

At once ingenious and ingenuous, this Panglossian reasoning reveals the shortcomings of what might be called a conjectural ecology. My Jivaro friends used to say, with a touch of exaggeration, that the sloth could go an entire lunar month without defecating, a periodicity that more fussy naturalists reduce to one week. Even while taking into account its reduced mobility, one can thus question that this paragon of continence might be able to contribute by its excretions to a significant enrichment of the soils over which it hangs. As for the causal relationship between this modest soil conditioner and monkey demographics, and between the latter and the dietary equilibrium of the Jivaro, I leave it to the reader to form his own opinion. Beyond its casual treatment of biological and ecological data, an approach of this kind testifies above all to a form of reductionism, extravagant in its project of subordinating the explanation of a social institution—a dietary taboo—to purely hypothetical interactions between non-human organisms. The object of study is claimed to be "cultural," to be a contingent rule specific to a particular society; however, the method of analysis denies the taboo this specificity by considering it ultimately as a functional response to a series of adaptive adjustments among animal and vegetal populations. It is thus to biology that the task of justifying the existence of a cultural phenomenon is given, but a biology that is in part imaginary, a blend of naïve teleology and semi-academic speculation, which evokes the naturalists of the Renaissance more than scientific ecology.

The riddles of culture are thus explained by natural causes, yet this postulate of ecological materialism, far from unsettling the respective jurisdictions of the sciences of nature and the sciences of culture, reinforces instead the separation of methods upon which the distinction within these disciplines is founded. Because of its intellectual origins in late-nineteenth century Germany, American anthropology elected early on to treat cultural realities as sui generis phenomena, expressed in singular languages and following singular historical trajectories, answerable in that regard to an internal interpretation that bears the mark of systematic relativism. It is the critique of this relativism that animates Harris' fight for a truly scientific approach to culture, and not any questioning of the legitimacy of the dualism between nature and society: for him, the study of culture is indeed the task of anthropology, seconded by the natural sciences from which it borrows some of its thought processes. In sum, the epistemological tension between the sciences and the humanities may have shifted somewhat within American anthropology, yet without affecting the understanding this discipline has of its object of study, or the largely implicit gnoseology which organizes the ways it captures it.

The two natures of Lévi-Strauss

Let us now return to Lévi-Strauss' argument. Far from advocating an uncompromising "mentalism," as Harris has accused him of, Lévi-Strauss personifies a naturalist approach much more radical than the one defended by the partisans of ecological determinism. It is in truth not the same nature: That of Harris is constituted by the sum of constraints that a geographical environment allegedly exerts on the development of social life, while that of Lévi-Strauss refers in the first instance to the organic mechanisms of human cognition. In the first case, nature is the ensemble of non-humans influence over humans; in the second, nature is the biological framework of the human condition. In fact, Lévi-Strauss is little interested in the first definition of nature, as the material substratum with which societies have to accommodate; according to him, the study of this aspect of reality concerns ethnography, history and cultural technology, but not structural anthropology, which focuses above all on the study of ideologies, understood here as systems of ideas. He has never faltered, however, in his conviction that the biological nature of humans conditions the intellectual operations through which culture receives an empirical content, even forming the hope that the interpretation of the productions of the mind might one day rest solely on brain physiology—a physicalist profession of faith which, as one can easily see, is of a materialism incomparably more radical than that of Harris. In the work of Lévi-Strauss, this resulted in a curious combination between, on the one hand, a declared lack of interest in what he called in Marxian terms "the order of infrastructures"—the institutional and technical organization of the flow of materials—and on the other, a theory of knowledge for which he claimed full responsibility and which turned its back on ordinary cognitive realism by highlighting the fact that the mind simultaneously gives meaning to the world and is a part, even a consequence, of that same world.

The Gildersleeve lecture offers an eloquent illustration of this paradoxical marriage between a form of idealism and a form of materialism. Faithful to his personal gnoseology, Lévi-Strauss rejects the opposition between mind and matter, and substitutes it with the reputedly equal interplay of two determinisms that operate simultaneously and in a complementary manner: one, of a techno-economic type, imposes upon the mind the constraints resulting from the relationship a society maintains with a particular environment; the other is a manifestation of the requirements inherent to the functioning of the mind, and it therefore has a universal impact. Understanding the functioning of the first type of determinism requires a good knowledge of the objective characteristics of natural objects which the mind selects in a given cultural context in order to constitute them into signifying ensembles: to elucidate the role played by a certain bird in a certain myth, one must know as much as possible about the former in order to understand why such-and-such morphological or behavioral trait has been selected to illustrate such-and-such property that the myth stages. We know that Lévi-Strauss has always taken great care to inform himself as thoroughly as possible about the fauna, flora, and geography of the populations whose myths he was studying. This knowledge is essential to establish how neighboring societies use different characteristics of the local environment to fulfill equivalent mythical functions. But what primarily interested Lévi-Strauss was discovering the laws of thought, therefore the second type of determinism—the one that affords an understanding of how the mind operates in different linguistic and geographical contexts, where it is constrained by the local particularities of the physical and social environment in its choice of working materials. Myths offer a privileged terrain for the study of mental determinism thus understood because, as they do not have the function of representing an exterior reality objectively, they can reveal with particular acuity the operations of a mind that takes itself as an object of thought.

The symmetry of mental determinism and environmental determinism that Lévi-Strauss strongly affirmed in the Gildersleeve lecture is thus largely an illusion. The physical environment ultimately has a very secondary function in his work, that of supplying mythic thought with natural objects the properties of which are good to symbolize, a function no doubt useful, but which understandably underwhelmed the enthusiasts of practical causality à la Marvin Harris. The indifference displayed by Lévi-Strauss towards the effect of ecological factors on the organization of social life provides a counterpart to his assertion of being interested solely in the study of "superstructures" as an extension, he argued, of what Marx had only sketched out. Thus formulated, this choice confirms the dissociation between material activity and its constraints on the one hand and the symbolic framework of this activity on the other, a dissociation which Lévi-Strauss attempted to eschew by advocating a monistic theory of knowledge in which the properties of the cosmos and the states of subjectivity would echo one another. Thus raised to the level of superstructures, nature becomes like a storehouse of sensible qualities from which the mind draws some elements to be transformed into signs, a nature "good to think" according to Lévi-Strauss' famous formula, but hardly more than that. This passive and richly illustrated nature that one browses like a treatise on botany or zoology is evidently not the hyperactive, invasive and almost teleological nature fancifully depicted by geographical determinism. But it is not either the other nature to which Lévi-Strauss often refers, the organic nature of our species, which guarantees the homogeneity of mental processes in all humans, holding out the promise that we will one day be able to elucidate their mechanisms. While nature as a collection of non-humans is reduced to a marginal position—that of fueling thought—the organic nature of humans becomes endowed with an eminent function, that of structuring the operations of the mind in resonance with the properties of matter. For Lévi-Strauss, the structural properties of the reality external to humans are no different from the codes by means of which the nervous system deciphers these properties, nor from the categories used by the intellect to account for the characteristics of physical objects. In short, he writes in the Gildersleeve lecture, "the mind, when trying to understanding it [the world], only applies operations which do not differ in kind from those going on in the natural world itself."

This physicalist theory of knowledge which unhesitatingly naturalizes the process itself of meaning-making enables Lévi-Strauss to reject all philosophical dualism, without preventing him nonetheless from implementing a perfect methodological dualism. Indeed, in his analyses of myths the physical environment is not treated "in nature," that is to say as an ensemble of causal effects, structural properties and molecular assemblages to be codified, decoded and recombined by the machinery of cognition and perception. Such an approach would require scientific tools that we are still far from possessing. The nature external to humans is rather hypostasized as a sort of lexicon of distinctive traits which the organs of the senses and the brain use to produce texts according to their own syntax. And if the analysis of myths is ultimately possible, it is precisely because the lexicon of non-human natures varies according to the environments that each culture must contend with, while the natural grammar of understanding that organizes these elements into discourse remains, for its part, invariant. Hence the paradox of structural anthropology that creates out of a monist conception of the mind and of the world the grounds for a method of analysis in which natural relativism – the variety of environments—plays a role elsewhere allotted to cultural relativism. One can see that, contrary to the critics that were leveled at him, notably in the United States, Lévi-Strauss is not a simple-minded dualist who allegedly has dedicated his work to the dissociation of nature and culture, of body and mind, of intellect and sentiments, willfully reifying the thought and institutions of peoples without writing by means of binary oppositions that are as abstract as they are unverifiable. To find examples of a literal use of the opposition between nature and culture, one should look not to Lévi-Stauss' work so much as to that of other authors—ethnologists or historians—who have been influenced by him and who have applied as recipes some of the elementary procedures of structural analysis without really appreciating the extent to which this approach is inseparable from a monist theory of knowledge which partly cancels out the dualism of the method.

I will give but one illustration of this trend, purposefully selected from within British anthropology. Within Britain, the Lévi-Straussian project was perceived as a way to escape the functionalism of Durkheimian sociology without renouncing the principles upon which it was founded. In "Belief and the Problem of Women" (1972), an article made famous by the controversy it caused among feminists, Edwin Ardener developed the idea, fairly new in the early 1970s, that the point of view of women was barely present in the ethnological literature due to the fact that the informants of ethnographers of either sex were most often men. Building a generalized argument from the example of the Bakweri of Cameroun, Ardener noted that the voice of women was made all the more inaudible because their cosmology was difficult for ethnographers to accept. By contrast with men, who represented society as an autonomous totality that clearly stands out from nature, and who therefore enjoyed holding forth on the institutions and rules of the domain they control, women would tend to situate themselves at the margin of the masculine and social sphere, in a zone of interface between the wilderness and the world of the village. Ardener claimed to be a follower of Lévi-Strauss, yet he reproached him for doubting that the opposition between nature and culture could be deeply seated in the order of things. For the British anthropologist, on the contrary, this opposition had an objective foundation: it was the result of the logical necessity of tallying two types of divides between different anatomical structures—the difference between the sexes and the difference between humans and non-humans. Hence the common equation, according to Ardener, between women and nature on the one hand, and the masculine world and culture on the other, a differentiation homologous to that between the self and the non-self, the familiar and the wild, the insider and the outsider. Analyses of this sort are too widespread to dwell on. Having retained from structuralism only a process of attractive simplicity, those who resort to it believe themselves unbound from the obligation to account for the complexity of the real world, so long as they have distributed objects, persons, attributes and relationship in a two-column table. These dichotomies then become substantive and fore-close any subtle appreciation of how the most diverse societies have organized the distinctive oppositions by means of which they mediate their relationship with the world and with others.

2
Anthropological Dualism

Why have I given such close attention to the controversy opposing "materialism" and "mentalism" in anthropology—to take up the simplistic terminology that was once in force in the United States? In so doing, am I not harping on a past phase of a discipline that has since found the intellectual means to overcome its impasses? By no means. Naturalist reductionism and semiological idealism are still alive and kicking, and they continue to form the two poles of an epistemological continuum along which everyone endeavoring to better understand the relationships between humans and non-humans must be positioned. It is true that hardly anyone occupies the extreme ends of the spectrum, especially in France where geographical possibilism has had a lasting influence on the way the social sciences conceive of the relationships between societies and their environments. Yet the two poles of the controversy have the merit of showing with particular

clarity the contradictions plaguing anthropology insofar as it posits that the world can be divided into two
separate fields of phenomena the interdependence of
which it is then necessary to show. At one end of the
spectrum, some will affirm that culture is a product of
nature, a convenient umbrella term under which one
can gather pell-mell cognitive universals, genetic determinations, physiological needs, or geographical
constraints. At the opposite end, others will forcefully
claim that, if left to itself, nature is always mute, even
unknowable in itself; that it comes into existence as a
relevant reality only when translated into the signs and
symbols that culture attaches to it.

Nature naturing, nature natured

If one wishes to lend this alternative a more evocative
force, one may resort to the distinction between "nature
naturing" and "nature natured" (*natura naturans,
natura naturata*) which Spinoza used to evidence the
connections between God as a cause of all things on the
one hand, and the totality of processes, objects, and
means of understanding them flowing from this imper-
sonal authority on the other. This pair of concepts
allowed Spinoza to draw an opposition between
"nature naturing" as a source of absolute determination, and "nature natured" as the actualization of this
determination in ways of being, thinking, and acting
which can be studied independently from their
supposed causal source. However, a drawback of char-
acterizing the state of a problem in terms of two
extreme ends of a polemical opposition is that the

method seems to exclude the intermediary states, the compromises, the different forms of conciliation. Yet between the rigorous naturalists of nature naturing and the staunch culturalists of nature natured, one might attempt to follow the narrow path that conjoins the two sides, despite its pitfalls since it is only too easy to slip to one side or the other.

Many geographers, sociologists, anthropologists and philosophers have strived to find a dialectical move that would allow them to sidestep the confrontation between these two dogmatisms. Some scholars, like Maurice Godelier in *The Mental and the Material*, have endeavored to couple "the mental and the material" in the analysis of the role of thought and physical realities in the production of social relationships. Others, such as Augustin Berque in *Médiance*, have outlined tools of environmental "trajectivity," that is to say the ability for environments to be understood as simultaneously objective and subjective realities. Yet others have endeavored, as I myself have done previously (*In the Society of Nature*), to explore the twists and turns of a "domestic nature," that is to say, a nature perceived and lived according to the principles that organize social life. But such efforts of mediation can only be in vain since they ultimately amount to stitching very coarsely the two sections of the world that our dualist cosmology had separated, the ostensible scar left by the suture emphasizing the dissociation rather than dissolving it. One can't see how such a compromise could be successfully achieved so long as we continue to subscribe to the presupposition upon which this cosmology is founded, namely the existence of a universal nature that is coded, or adapted to, by a multitude of heterogeneous cultures. On the axis that leads from a completely natural culture to a completely cultural nature, one can never find a point of equilibrium, only compromises that are closer to one pole or the other. Such is the problem that anthropology, the daughter of modern thought, has found in its cradle and has attempted to resolve ever since so that, to take up a metaphor developed by Marshall Sahlins in *Culture and Practical Reason*, this science finds itself like a prisoner compelled for over a century to pace its cell, confined within the walls of intellectual constraints and practical determinations.

Make no mistake. These remarks are not meant to castigate our cosmology and to ascribe to it all the evils with which the Moderns are afflicted. The dualism of nature and culture is only one way among others of tracing the continuities and discontinuities in the fabric of the world and there is no reason to find it more unreasonable or arbitrary than any other ontological distribution. It has at least had the virtue of delimiting clearly a domain of positivity for the social sciences, something which had been achieved nowhere else before, and of making possible attempts to supersede it such as the one I am presently undertaking. This being said, such a heritage greatly complicates the task of anthropology which is, preeminently, to understand how people who do not share our cosmology could have invented realities distinct from our own, manifesting a creativity that should never be measured in terms of our own accomplishments. But achieving this kind of understanding is something anthropology cannot do so long as it assumes that our own reality, our ways of establishing discontinuities and detecting stable relationships in the world, our manners of distributing entities and phenomena, processes and modes of action into categories which are allegedly predetermined by the texture and structure of things, are a universal fact of human experience. This incapacity is all the more paradoxical insofar as anthropology has never ceased to proclaim its methodological relativism, declaring judiciously that the study of customs and institutions requires a suspension of judgment and demands—first and foremost, that one not take the social norms current in the place of origin of the observer as the standard against which to measure the distance separating it from the other norms.

A peculiar timidity, however, takes hold of anthropology when the moment comes to extend this methodological skepticism to our own cosmology, either because it is thought implicitly that it is shared by all and that humans everywhere can distinguish between a matter of nature and a matter of society, or because it is believed that the dissociation between these two orders of phenomena is a scientific tool as transhistorical as the periodic table of the elements. But this is wrong on both counts: only in the last third of the nineteenth century did the dualism of nature and culture take shape in Europe as an epistemological device allowing a simultaneous discrimination between distinct orders of phenomena and distinct means of knowing about them. Admittedly, the idea of nature took its first faltering steps in ancient Greece and formed the pivot around which the scientific revolution unfolded during the seventeenth century. This revolution legitimized the idea of a mechanical nature, where the behavior of each element can be accounted for by laws within a totality understood as the sum of the parts and interactions of these elements. But opposite this nature, at once an autonomous ontological domain, a field of inquiry and of scientific experimentation, an object inviting practical exploitation and amelioration, there was not yet a collective counterpart. For singular communities, differentiated by customs, language, and relations—what we now term "cultures" —to emerge as scientific objects susceptible of being opposed to the field of natural regularities, it was necessary to wait until the end of the nineteenth century and the intense debates that, particularly in Germany with philosophers like Heinrich Rickert, lead to the distinction between the methods and objects of the sciences of nature and the sciences of culture. There is therefore nothing universal about this contrast. Nor is there either anything properly demonstrable about it. Distinguishing among the objects of the world those that are a matter of human intentionality and those that stem from the universal laws of matter and of life is an ontological operation, a hypothesis and a choice with regard to the relations that beings maintain with one another as a result of the qualities which are ascribed to them. Neither physics, nor chemistry, nor biology can provide proof of this, and it is furthermore extremely rare that the practitioner of these sciences, in their everyday use, actually refer to the abstraction that is nature as their domain of investigation. (I explore these issues in Chapter 3 of my book, *Beyond Nature and Culture*.)

Anthropology, no doubt because it is in great part the daughter of philosophy, has thus been averse to questioning the universality of the Modern cosmology. It is true that is has not gone so far as to claim that all cosmologies are similar to ours—this would not be very plausible. Simply, we see others, the non-moderns, through the distorting lens that structures our own cosmology, and thus as so many singular expressions of culture in contrast with a unique and universal nature. In other words, we do not envision non-Western civilizations, or even pre-modern Western ones, as complete systems of conceptualization of the world alternative to our own, but as more or less exotic ways of accounting for the state of a world that our own system of conceptualization has established (this idea was brilliantly developed by Roy Wagner in *The Invention of Culture*). Making modern dualism the template for all the states of the world has thus lead anthropology to a particular form of academic eurocentrism, which consists in believing not that the realities that humans objectivize are everywhere identical, but that our own manner of objectivizing is universally shared.

Following these somewhat general epistemological considerations, let us now examine the concrete consequences of the dualism of nature and culture on the actual practice of anthropology. Let me first emphasize that if controversies of the kind that opposed Marvin Harris and Claude Lévi-Strauss are at all possible, it is because they rest on a background of shared habits of thoughts and references constituting the common ground from which oppositions can emerge. In other words, for all the vigor of the theoretical divergences running through the discipline, they clearly reveal the convergence of their premises as soon as they are put back within the modern cosmological frame from which they originated. Admittedly, the diverse approaches seem at first sight to be distributed on either sides of the spectrum going from nature naturing to nature natured. But because the existence of this spectrum is never questioned, it is in fact the same network of presuppositions which informs divergent positions. These presuppositions influence the whole of the anthropological approach, but they are most notable in the following three stages: in the characterization of its object; in the determination of its methods; and in the definition of the type of knowledge that it produces. At the risk of trying the patience of the reader with yet another discussion of academic schools of thought, it is thus necessary to examine and discuss the different propositions, to highlight the hidden clauses and surreptitious affinities, in short, to clear away the bases in order to build with more confidence. In anthropology as in the other social sciences, any reform of the analytical framework of a discipline requires a reflective reappraisal of the manner in which it constructs knowledge and of the theories that purport to account for this operation. As Bourdieu expressed it in *Outline of a Theory of Practice*: "epistemological reflection on the conditions of possibility of anthropological science is an integral part of anthropological science."

A paradoxical object

Anthropology defines its object of study, Culture or cultures, as the system of mediation with Nature invented by humanity, a distinctive attribute of *Homo sapiens* which includes technical ability, language, symbolic activity and the capacity to assemble in collectivities that are partly freed from biological legacies. Despite being rarely formulated in such an explicit way, such a definition nonetheless remains widely shared. This definition is quite manifest in the writings of certain authors who claim to adhere to materialism and who, while conceiving culture as an apparatus of adaptation to nature, will willingly recognize that the latter cannot be known except through the mechanisms of the former. One can count among such authors some followers of ecological or technical determinism, including Leslie White who, in a lecture entitled "Man, Culture, and Human Beings," described the earliest times of humanity in these terms: "Between Man and nature hung the veil of culture, and he could see nothing save through this medium." One also finds among them authors who invoke the preeminence of utilitarian functions in the structuring of social life and think, like Malinowski, in *A Scientific Theory of Culture*, that "every cultural achievement that implies the use of artifacts and symbolism is an instrumental enhancement of human anatomy." Lastly, one finds among them those who, like Maurice Godelier—here in *The Mental and the Material*—hold as the central tenet of their work the fact that "Man has a history because he transforms nature."

This conception of anthropology, however, is not exclusive to the materialists. The idea that the necessity of inventing an original response to organic and environmental constraints is peculiar to humans proves to be equally common among those who are principally concerned with the symbolic dimensions of culture. Think of Lévi-Strauss, who credits Rousseau with having founded the field of ethnology by posing the problem of the relations between nature and culture —a point of view echoed by Michel Foucault when he wrote, in *The Order of Things*: "the general problem of all ethnology is indeed that of the relations (of continuity and of discontinuity) between nature and culture." Think of Clifford Geertz, a talented advocate of hermeneutical anthropology, who nevertheless declared boldly: "an established society is the end point of such a long history of adaptation to its environment that it has, as it were, made of that environment a dimension of itself" (in "The Wet and the Dry"). As for Mary Douglas, she showed a less nuanced dualism by asserting: "The scientists find out true, objective things about physical nature. The human society invests these findings with social meanings" (*Implicit meanings*). I do not exclude myself from the lot, having written some rather similar things: "the principles of the construction of social reality are primarily to be sought in the relations between human beings and their natural environment"—this from "Societies of nature and the nature of society."

To pursue this list of quotations would be fastidious and above all useless. There is an implicit agreement over the fact that the domain of anthropology is that which articulates the universal determinations imposed by the laws of matter and of life with the conventions invented by humans in order to organize their common existence, the domain in which the necessity for humans to interact with non-humans on a daily basis, notably to ensure their subsistence, intersects with the possibility for them to endow these interactions with a multitude of diverse meanings. If anthropology was able to conquer its autonomy, it was because it defended the idea that all societies are compromises between nature and culture, and that it is thus imperative for a specialized discipline to examine the variety of expressions of this compromise in order to propose the generative laws and the grammar of these combinations. In short, a dual world is the constitutive dimension of the object of anthropology. One could even say that this science was born as a response to the challenge of reducing the gap between the two orders of reality just established by the theory of knowledge in the second half of the nineteenth century. The duality of the field of meaning built into the definition of the object of anthropology could not but find its way into the manner in which it is approached. If an agreement exists on the fact that human experience is conditioned by the coexistence of two fields of phenomena ruled by distinct principles, tackling their interface becomes inevitable, taking as a starting point one aspect or the other: either the determinations that the use, control or transformation of nature induce, universal determinations whose effect are particularized by singular environments, techniques and social systems; or the particularities of the symbolic treatment of a nature homogeneous in its frontiers and its mode of functioning, particularities that are recurrent because of the universality of the mechanisms mobilized and the uniqueness of the object to which they apply.

The two approaches draw their conceptual resources from respectable philosophical antecedents.

In fact, they both almost always situate themselves, ·
sometimes without even knowing it, in terms of a given
moment in the work of Marx. The partisans of nature
natured thus identify with the first Marx, the one from
his juvenilia still permeated with Hegelian dialectics.
This is the Marx who is interested in a nature human-
ized and historicized by praxis, the "second nature" of
that philosophical tradition, at once conditioned by the
formative activity of humans and in part differentiated
from them by its own determinations. It is that Marx
who wrote in Paris in 1844: "Only here has the natural
existence of man become his human existence, and
nature become human."

No one better than Marshall Sahlins has
known how to make the most of the Marxian idea that,
when taken in isolation and as an abstraction, nature is
deprived of all meaning, even of all utility, for humans.
He expressed this forcefully when he wrote: "nature is
to culture as the constituted is to the constituting.
Culture is not only nature expressed in another form.
Rather the reverse: the action of nature unfolds in the
terms of culture; that is, in a form no longer its own
but embodied as meaning." This approach is rather
different from that of Mary Douglas to whom he is
often compared. Faithful to the Durkheimian tradition, Douglas still differentiated the objective properties of nature, the classificatory and moral use that
culture makes of them, and the effect social categories
have in turn on the construction of representations of
the non-human environment. Sahlins, by contrast, is
inscribed as much in the North-American culturalist
tradition as in the direct line of the younger Marx
when he challenges the possibility of understanding
nature as a thing in itself upon which social values

would be projected *a posteriori*, and when he concedes to the sole symbolic function the power of making the physical world into a reality that can be represented and exploited by humans. Here we have a vigorous critique, even a reversal, of the utilitarian logic so commonly invoked by the tenants of nature naturing. To be sure, modes of using and representing the environment are indeed subordinated to a certain form of practical interest, yet the latter can only be expressed through the filter that each cultural system imposes upon it according to the ends it pursues. In other words, it is culture that defines both what nature is to humans and the manner in which a given society takes advantage of it according to the preferences dictated by local practices.

Sahlins' position, at least in the 1970s, is thus paradoxical. On the one hand, he identifies with great lucidity the problem which anthropology has never ceased to confront and from which it draws in great part its *raison d'être*: accounting for the functional relations between domains that were originally posited as separated by an analytical distinction that was ratified without discussion because it drew its strength from the obviousness of the model that our own society presented. Furthermore, Sahlins uses this same polarity to critique utilitarian reason. It is culture that encompasses nature and determines its modes of expression, it is through the first that all societies were able to objectivize images more or less similar to what we know of the second. The logical consequence of this approach— and I have myself learned the lesson—can only be to forsake the idea of formulating the problem of anthropology in terms of nature and culture so much do these notions taint the problem itself with eurocentrism. This is what Sahlins has done with no hesitation in *The Western Illusion of Human Nature*: "As enchanted as our universe may still be, it is also still ordered by a distinction of culture and nature that is evident to virtually no one else but ourselves." With this requiem for the hypostasis of culture, a century of North-American anthropology comes to an end.

The apostles of nature naturing, for their part, rely instead on a simplification of Marx's mature work, on the Marx of the consolidation of historical materialism who seems to take interest in nature solely as a precondition of economic activity. The socialization of this nature, made once again autonomous, is only considered in a partial and finalized manner. At the level of productive forces it becomes a physical given mediated by tools and skills, confined to a subaltern role by the privilege conceded to technology of bringing to light the structure of the modes of production and the course of their evolution. At the level of the relations of production, it is limited to the resources that can be converted into use value or exchange value because they constitute, in a given era, the means of labor. Analytically, nature finds itself cleaved: from the material point of view, it is no more than one of the components allowing the satisfaction of needs; from a social point of view, it is no more than one of the elements that conditions the shape of the relationships that men weave between themselves. To approach the objectification of the non-human domain as a consequence of the production of the means of subsistence and wealth is thus a prejudice evenly shared, and it would have been surprising if anthropology did not inherit it. Its effects can be felt as much in the technological determinism of a White or a Steward as in the far more common prejudice that the ideas organizing the use of nature are the ideological by-product of a supposedly objective practice. Were we to restore its purity to practice—its rationality, its purpose, its function—the clouds of representation would dissipate, reduced to the transparent veil of false-consciousness. The vast majority of contemporary anthropology still deludes itself with this sweet and messianic illusion.

Controversies and convergences

By defining its object as a mixture of Nature and cultures, anthropology was constrained to glean from the methods developed by other sciences thought to be better prepared to tackle one face or the other of the Janus it had taken as its subject. Unfortunately, the borrowing has most often resulted in an impoverishment and a simplification of the borrowed explanatory model.

The path of reduction

The naturalist current has embraced the different variations of determinism, with a marked preference for final causes. The outline of an anthropology of needs provided by Malinowski in *A Scientific Theory of Culture* offers an appropriate example of this tendency, all the more distressing in that it contrasts severely with the refinement and depths of the ethnographic analyses that the founder of modern ethnology has given in his monographs. Malinowski postulated a continuum between the natural and the cultural, the organic and the superorganic, thus relying on biology by drawing inspiration from its methods. Anthropology, as a science of culture, has accordingly the task of exploring the institutional forms which, at all times and in all places, constitute so many adaptive responses to the biological determinism of human nature, primarily those responses which allow for the satisfaction of "elementary needs." Thus, the production of subsistence is considered to be a response to metabolic needs; kinship, to reproductive needs; shelter, to needs for corporeal well-being, etc. Such responses are hardly enlightening because, even at the high level of generality at which Malinowski is located, each one of them can correspond to several needs, and each need can generate several responses. Hygiene and protection are just as adequate answers to the need for corporeal well-being as shelter, while the functions of protection and shelter serve to ensure health as much as corporeal well-being and safety. When they are viewed solely in terms of their functional aspect, so-called cultural institutions can only be polyvalent and the biological needs they serve are themselves inextricably entangled.

Yet Malinowski is too good an ethnographer not to understand that a simple causal relation between natural constraints and their cultural responses hardly allows for an explanation of the function of a whole ensemble of institutions so particularized that they cannot be determined only by the biological substrate. Beyond the primary needs, conditioned by the nature of humans and by the ecological characteristics of the environment in which they evolve, "secondary needs" thus come into play. These stem from the specifications that social life imposes upon the cultural responses created by primary needs, and they generate in turn new cultural responses—economy as a means of ensuring subsistence production, for example, or customs, traditions, symbolic practices and language as instruments of collective solidarity. Here again, the characterization of needs appears, against all logic, as an *a posteriori* functional justification of the responses that they provoke, the nature of the cause being presupposed by the definition of the effect.

Malinowski's incapacity to work backwards from the social fact to its organic foundation is a constitutive aspect of all functional finalism, because the more general the hypothetical need placed at the origin of an institution, the less explanatory value it has. Correlatively, the more undetermined by its generality the need is, the larger will be the sample of cultural practices that, within a same society, can claim to answer to it. When the naturalist explanation associates different cultural manifestations with a unique posited need, it does no more than assert the necessity of culture as a means of translating that need. This truism conceals an inability to account for the content of social institutions. It is a truism to assert that the construction of shelter answers the needs of well-being or protection, but one can hardly see what one could say about, for instance, gothic architecture, by invoking only these needs. The critique is equally valid for the more recent instantiations of biological reductionism: human sociobiology, for example, and its ambition to explain social behavior in terms of coefficients of genetic relationships, or optimal foraging theory that sees in the optimization of hunting and gathering routes the result of an adaptive evolution determined by natural selection. Because they make their explanation of culture depend on a metamorphosed natural potentiality—instinct, altruism or genetic adaptation—that they isolate by induction, all these approaches seem condemned to oscillate between teleological arguments and tautological claims.

Cultural ecology has ventured into the same type of impasse when it has taken from biology one of its vaguest concepts, as well as one of the most loaded with finalism: namely, adaptation. Roy Rappaport, no doubt the most subtle among the theoreticians of this school of thought, has sought, in *Ecology, Meaning and Religion*, to sidestep the problem by distinguishing between two ways of accounting for the adaptive function of an institution: explanation by the formal cause and explanation by the final cause. The first type of explanation consists in establishing the formal characteristics of an institution which render it capable of fulfilling the specific functions that is recognized for it in all the systems in which it is present. But the broad generality imposed by this definition reduces the object upon which the method could be applied to a small number of formal properties within a reduced range of social institutions. The latter are indeed limited to what Marxist terminology calls instances: politics, economics, kinship, or magic/religion. It is evident that these instances have formal properties that are adequate to the function they fulfill, and the explanation by formal cause thus defined can only lead to truisms. The explanation by final cause is by contrast always singular, since it aims to specify the function of an element within a given system by demonstrating its contribution to the survival or reproduction of this system. Such an explanation can never be generalized because different elements can fulfill the same function in different systems, in the same way an element can fulfill distinct

functions in different systems. What the explanation by
final causes is attempting to pass as a necessary causal
relationship is nothing more than the assertion of a
simple compatibility between a cultural form and a
biological function. Oscillating between a tautological
formal cause and a teleological final cause, cultural ecology does not escape from the dilemma in which
Malinowski's reductionism was trapped.

The path of translation

The idea that nature is an independent instance the
internal organization and limits of which are everywhere and always identical, has distinct effects on those
who are interested in the semantic rather than in the
practical dimensions of culture. A universal natural
order indeed becomes the only basis which guarantees
the possibility of translating and interpreting the understanding another person has of reality, either because
this Other perceives and parcels out a world structured
like mine, using the same mechanisms as those that
govern my own apperception and my cognitive treatment of the subdivisions of that world, or because the
existence of a same phenomenological referent is
deemed indispensable for evaluating and understanding
the very diverse systems of denotations that this referent calls forth. The difference between the two
branches of this alternative might seem considerable
since it is this difference which separates the
Universalists from the Relativists in the field of the
ethnosciences. It becomes less significant, however, if
one considers that the study of so-called folk knowledge and classifications bears upon objects reputed to
be "natural" by them both. The first stress that

taxonomies of fauna and flora possess everywhere the same internal architecture, while the second insist upon the measure of creativity that each culture injects into the semantic ordering of the animal and vegetal world. But neither of them question the received knowledge particular to the modern cosmology that nature is an ontologically discrete domain with stable frontiers.

Brent Berlin, the principal figure of contemporary ethnobiological studies, has expressed without ambiguity a universalist point of view on the matter. Contrary to what the pioneers of ethnoscience of the Yale school had maintained, Berlin argued in *Ethnobiological Classification* that folk classifications of plants and animals are not cultural constructions that depend upon context, but exact translations of what is perceived in nature: "humans are everywhere constrained essentially in the same way—by nature's basic plan—in their conceptual recognition of the biological diversity of their natural environments." Berlin concedes that social organization, rituals, religious beliefs, or aesthetics can be singular productions relative to each culture; on the other hand, as soon as perceiving and naming groups of plants and animals is involved, "humans... do not construct an order, they discern it." Nature thus offers itself to the experience of the senses as a discrete set of discontinuities the structure of which is identically perceived in all cultures, even if all do not exhaust these discontinuities to the same degree in their classifications. The taxonomical structure of organisms takes the form of a hierarchy which includes named categories, the taxa, and whose most complete form comprises six ranks: kingdom, form of life, intermediary level, genus, species, and variety.

To those who might think that such an architecture is derived from the organization of classes in
Western systematics, the tenants of ethnobiological
universalim such as Scott Atran retort that the opposite
is true: the principles of Linnaean taxonomy, like those
of any other taxonomy of organisms, are based on the
common sense observation of the natural world, hence
the structural similarities among all systems of classification of fauna and flora. The natural order is presupposed since it always proceeds from the rules and mechanisms that modern biology has brought to light. As
concerns the universality of common sense, it is guar-
anteed either by an innate human aptitude to distinguish "natural kinds" from all other percepts, or by a
tendency of the mind to select as typical representations, or "natural prototypes," certain members of a
biological taxon which reputedly constitute the focus of
a category because of their perceptive salience. In every
case, the categorization of plants and animals is deemed
to be a "natural" process since it matches a natural
structure of the biological world—the segmentation in
species—with a natural device of the cognitive system.

In sum, in ethnobiological classification, as in
medieval theology, Nature is a great book that all,
learned or illiterate, are equally able to decipher, recog-
nizing in it if not the same words, at least the same division into sentences, paragraphs and chapters. Perhaps
we should even say that the book is everywhere written
in the same alphabet. According to Berlin, "ethnobiological nomenclature represents a *natural system of
naming* very revealing of the way in which people
conceptualize living objects in their environment" (the
emphasis is added). It is no longer solely the categorization as a cognitive and perceptive operation which

is here naturalized, but the linguistic mechanisms by means of which it is expressed. In this domain, the motivation of the signifier by the signified is attested by the oft-noted fact that the names given to plants and animals make ample metaphorical use of the traits characteristic of the morphology, behavior or habitat of the organisms that they designate. It would come also and above all from the fact that an entire segment of ethnobiological nomenclatures at the generic level is "transparent" as far as semantics is concerned, in that it purportedly reflects psychological associations between meaning and sound. Thus, phonemes with a high acoustic frequency evoke sudden and rapid movements, and are most common in names for birds, while phonemes with a low acoustic frequency, which evoke slow and continuous movements, are typical of names for fish.

In contrast with Roman Jakobson from whom he claims to draw his insight, and who interprets the motivated correspondences between sound and meaning within the system of distinctive oppositions of a given language and not according to the acoustic properties of such or such a phoneme taken in isolation, Berlin takes sound motivation to be an *a priori* universal characteristic of ethnobiological nomenclatures. Yet, as Lévi-Strauss aptly remarked in a commentary of Jakobson's work (in *Le regard éloigné*), while the arbitrariness of the linguistic sign can be questioned once the sign is constituted within a particular semantic environment and influenced by it, this arbitrariness remains indubitable "when one adopts the point of view of resemblance, that is to say when one compares the signifiers of a same signified in many different languages." By turning a domain of linguistic activity into a system of quasi-automatic denotations which translates natural constraints that are exerted in the same manner everywhere and always, Berlin squarely places himself in the straight line of the Thomist theory of abstraction: "*nomina debent naturae rerum congruere*," names should fit with nature.

The Relativists Berlin aims to refute had in fact already offered the outline of this denotative conception of the classification of natural objects. When they began in the United States in the 1950s, studies of "ethnosciences" had the ambition of comparing the mental procedures that different peoples implement in organizing their environment, starting from the hypothesis that each cultural system operates according to its own cognitive system, each one unique because it is conditioned by the structures of a specific language. However, while the declared goal was indeed to study all the nuances and subtleties of cultural grammars, the latter were limited, in the most common definition, to the sum of the classification systems of a society, the analysis of the dynamic principles that structure social and symbolic physiology being *de facto* left to classic ethnology. Yet, the study of a culture understood as the study of the morphology of its classification systems presupposes that one can determine, in a non-arbitrary manner, the semantic boundaries of the categories that it uses, in other words how a field of objects is circumscribed by language without relying on an *a priori* definition of this domain. It is a matter of ensuring that a collection of lexemes gathered by an observer indeed constitutes, for the speakers of the language, a classification which divides a part of phenomenological experience into a discrete semantic field.

The method advocated by ethnoscience consists of isolating named categories, groupings of objects distinguished by lexemes, and of attempting to understand how these categories are organized within a field of contrast reputed to refer to a domain of reality culturally relevant for the society considered. The constitution of the field of contrast must be such that each lexeme has at least one definitional trait in common with all the others—a trait that characterizes the domain of referents on which the lexeme depends and which authorizes, in the natural context, its permutation with the other lexemes within the same field—and one distinctive trait which opposes the lexeme to all others that are related to it. Thus, "bean" and "carrot" are two lexemes belonging to the semantic field of vegetable names within the folk classification of plants in the English language, because they can be substituted for one another in utterances of this type: "I do not like carrot soup, I prefer bean soup;" while neither can be substituted to lexemes belonging to a different field of contrast—one cultivates carrots but not pianos, one shells beans but not the Holy Spirit.

The principle obstacle that this method of ethnosemantic analysis runs into is its inability to guarantee that a given field of contrasts actually coincides, for the speakers of a given language, with a conceptual field. While the discrimination between classes of related lexemes does not present major difficulties, especially in languages where nominal classifiers exist, the determination of fields of contrasts within the linguistic material, on the other hand, cannot unfailingly delineate a field of phenomenological experience, nor ensure that it has cognitive reality for the members of a given culture. Let us consider an apparently simple case; that of the semantics of names for color. In Jivaro Achuar, a South-American language, alongside lexemes that can be easily translated to English because they designate large bands of the spectrum which are divided in a manner more or less identical to our own nomenclature (*kɛaku*: red, *takump*: yellow, *puhu*: white, *šuwin*: black, etc.), one finds a series of words or expressions which serve, by metaphor or metonymy, to denote variations in intensity or tonality, variations which nothing allows to exclude *a priori* from the cultural domain of color among the Jivaro. These linguistic indicators bring out a field of contrasts different from that which defines the lexicon of colors. Thus, in the highly codified context of the poetic imagery unique to certain magical incantations, mentioning the swallow (*tchinímpi*) evokes a metallic shimmering, mentioning the toucan (*tsukaŋgá*) evokes the vibrancy of an intense yellow, while mentioning the anaconda (*paŋgi*) evokes the sheen of bronze. When these three animals—the lexemes for which belong in principle to the field of contrasts of ethnozoology— appear in a song, certain properties of their appearance stand out as pertinent semantic traits, these properties being themselves associated to a quality, a state, or an emotion: metallic shimmers denote invincibility, a pulsating yellow denotes love, bronze denotes evil. In short, there is here an overlap between several fields of contrast and it is not a semantic criterion internal to language which enables one to isolate the possible conceptual field to which all these denotations could refer, but rather a certain type of knowledge acquired by the observer when he interprets and relates statements produced in different contexts.

It is in great part to compensate for this difficulty that ethnoscience has made such liberal use of the famous distinction between etic and emic. These terms were fashioned by the linguist Kenneth Pike out of the suffixes of "phonetics" and "phonemics," in order to better distinguish between the approach centered on linguistic sounds and their notations as universal acoustic phenomena (phonetics) and the approach focusing on the phonemes of a particular language and in the relevant traits that characterize it (phonemics). By analogy with the study of linguistic sounds, the characteristics of physical reality considered independently from any cultural dimension can thus be defined as etic, while an emic approach aims, in the words of David French, "to discover and describe the behavioral system [of a given culture] in its own terms, identifying not only the structural units but also the structural classes to which they belong" In ethnoscience an emic description should thus be able to indicate what are, in the environment of a culture, the etic elements which are recognized by it and which it invests with a particular meaning.

But the environment of a culture is far more complex than the acoustic parameters of language, and it is impossible to study etic elements defined in abstraction from all cultural context, since it is according to the observer's own categories that they are isolated in the first place and deemed to be relevant prototypes of every system of knowledge in the world. An ethnobotanical survey, for example, requires to carry out as complete an inventory as possible of the local flora as an etic procedure preliminary to the emic analysis of the classifications and uses of plants by the people studied. The delimitation of the domain of study—botany as the specialized knowledge of plants—and its internal organization—nomenclature as the lexical expression of the discontinuity of species—is the product of a division of phenomenal reality long accepted in the West, not of a vantage point stripped of all cultural prejudice. The multiplication of ethnobotanical studies may well create the illusion that the domain to which they apply is of an etic type, since its content and its outline appear to be confirmed by the overlap or the convergence of the different emic descriptions given of them; but this experimental verification can never be anything but a confirmation of the presupposition that established the vegetal world as a specialized field of inquiry. Because they do not question the notion that an internal and external segmentation of the natural world constitutes the universal background against which cultural particularities can be evaluated, the Relativists prefigured the denotative conception of local knowledge that the Universalists defend. Here, the arbitrariness of the sign is not questioned, as it was by B. Berlin, but the demarcation of the semantic categories by means of which reality is grasped remains dependent upon a referent presented without discussion as transcending all cultural particularity.

In his defense of ethnoscience, William Sturtevant remarked that one task of this branch of ethnology "can be viewed as the solution of the old problem of translation." That might be so, on the condition however of clarifying that it is not a matter of simple translation of the culture of the observed into that of the observer—that commonplace of ethnology—but rather one of a bidirectional translation, the observer beginning by translating his culture into that of the observed by detecting in it a division of the world analogous to that which is familiar to him, before retranslating the observed culture in a language acceptable to his community of origin. Whether it constitutes the final term of the reduction which the naturalists aspire to achieve, or whether it is the object of a translation by ethnosemantics, it is always the same homogenous and autonomous natural order which guarantees the legitimacy of the knowledge produced by the analysts of culture. This shared presupposition induces a paradoxical chiasm between the methods and the results of the two approaches. The fetishization of adaptive constraints by ecological anthropology ultimately leads to particularism, each culture being a unique response to the singularities of its environment, while relativistic ethnoscience buttresses its descriptions of cultural classifications of nature with the presumed universality of the reality that they are supposed to account for. Each one ends up at a point from which the other believes to be departing, the analytical paths afforded by dualism hardly favoring innovations in the ways of understanding the customs of the world.

3
To Each His Own Nature

One might think that the preceding considerations give too much importance to questions of epistemology, whose influence on ethnographic practice might in fact be negligible. In the same way that molecular biology produces valid experimental results without burdening itself with an actual theory of life, so too could the descriptions and analyses of the institutions and customs of exotic peoples well do without a refined gnoseology and a reflexive methodology. Experience shows that a strong dose of empiricism, a touch of humility and a great deal of patience and intuition are, for the most part, the only baggage required to report with subtlety on the habits and customs of others. Besides, is it not the case that the ethnographers who have studied members of the same ethnic group at not too distant times produce reports that are roughly comparable, regardless of their theoretical inclinations, the measure of subjectivity attributable to each one and the vagaries of their research procedures? A ritual, a rule of marriage, a principle of filiation, a fishing technique or a system of exchange of goods do not vary according to those who witness them, and the analogous terms used by successive observers to describe them should constitute a sufficient guarantee that ethnology has steered clear of the crudest traps of ethnocentrism.

All of this is no doubt true so long as one sticks to the faithful description of a sequence of acts and words, of a publically formulated consensus rule, or of a corpus of pronouncements sanctioned by oral tradition. But an ethnographer is not a bailiff and he does more than send in reports. He interprets, that is to say that he gives meaning to enigmatic behaviors by attributing to others beliefs that are supposed to motivate those actions. If the observer necessarily invests these beliefs with a different content than that which characterizes his own beliefs—although he often assumes to have none— he confers on them, nevertheless, a status identical to that accorded to such representations within his community of origin. Said otherwise, beliefs are not considered as legitimate knowledge but rather as symbolic artifacts by means of which we believe that those who believe in them think they are able to act upon the world, a phenomenon which was brilliantly analyzed by Jean Pouillon. In the field, for example, the ethnographer will not resist making a distinction between the meteorological knowledge of a population, founded upon a long series of rigorous observations, and the rituals and magical invocations destined to make the rain come. The forecast of weather changes is often believed to be a knowledge of a positive nature— although it is often contradicted by facts—, that is to say a knowledge supposed to be true for the observed and verifiable for the observer, while rain-making rituals are by contrast believed to rest upon beliefs reputed to be objectively false (in that they go against the expectations of common sense and of scientific experiences), but subjectively true for those who carry out these ceremonies. In ethnographic inquiries, the dualism of nature and culture that the observer carries with him thus effectively compels him to approach the system of objectification of reality which he studies as a more or less impoverished variant of that which is familiar to us, the local system ultimately proving to be incapable of completely objectifying our own reality.

Truth and Beliefs

Anthropology has adopted three main strategies, sometimes combined in the work of a same author, to account for the lag between our cosmology and those of non-modern peoples. The most basic strategy consists in teasing out practical activity from the haze of beliefs and superstitions by which humans disguise the real conditions of their collective existence. While practice is assumed to rest on objective knowledge, effective techniques, and exact assessments of natural determinations, non-practical thought is judged to be a fantastical reflection of the relationships that individuals weave amongst themselves and with their environment—in short, an ideology. Because ethnologists have long concentrated on societies without classes or with little internal differentiation, the ideological superstructure does not function so much as a veil for still-embryonic forms of economic or political alienation, as it constitutes a mechanism ensuring the social integration and ecological adaptation of those who adhere to the system of values by which this ideology is expressed. Within this perspective, shared by certain Marxist authors, by the supporters of "cultural materialism," or by the advocates of utilitarianism, humans are above all beings of need, such that the main goal of their action upon the world can only be an instrumentalization of material reality through labor. Thanks to labor, humans extract their means of subsistence from their environment which they partially transform, metamorphosing themselves in the process in that they establish a social mediation with their fellow humans and with objects. In doing so, they objectify nature and convert it into a totality that is distinct from themselves. The primacy given to practice as the unique source of all positivity thus leads to isolating a world of "representations" which become either a deformed echo of constraints induced by the social use of natural resources, or a retroactive filter by the means of which pieces of reality and of human activity which would exist before and outside of all thought are brought into consciousness. For this type of anthropology, ethnography borders on uselessness since social actors, eternally ignorant of the motives that induce them to act, have only poor fables to offer to those who would be willing to listen to them.

Another, more charitable, approach sees the cosmologies and religious beliefs of non-modern peoples as systems of explanation of nature, no doubt erroneous in regard to the teachings of Science, yet testifying to an authentic desire to give order and logic to the world by detecting causal relationships between phenomena. In the most classic expression of this conception, advanced long ago (1933) by Evans-

Pritchard, traditional religion is, among other things, a mental model of the organization of the natural world and its dynamic principles, comparable in intention to modern science; a true theory that fosters among those who adhere to it behaviors aiming to exploit their cosmological knowledge for useful purposes. Magic is thus simply the practical translation of a system of beliefs bearing upon the nature of the physical world, and which exploits certain of its supposed properties to insure mastery over it; a form of instrumental action flowing from fallacious ideas yet faithful in its spirit to the operational efficacy of determinism. A more radical and older version of this approach, traditionally qualified as intellectualist, exemplified in James G. Frazer's *The Golden Bough*, has worked to justify the origin of magical or religious beliefs in terms of the function that they fulfill. Born from a need to understand natural phenomena and act upon them, these beliefs are hypotheses concerning the functioning of the world, entirely rational considering the context in which they were formulated. Timid anticipations of Science, nascent objectifications of the regularities observable in nature, non-modern cosmologies are thus distinguished from our own not by faults in their reasoning, but by an incapacity to discern these levels of phenomenal reality upon which a deterministic explanation can be legitimately applied.

Durkheim condemned the idea that traditional religions are rudimentary theories about the mechanisms of the physical world, proposing instead, in *The Elementary Forms of the Religious Life*, to see in them "a system of notions by the means of which individuals represent to themselves the society of which they are part, as well as the obscure but intimate relationships that they maintain with it." While the intellectualist approach emphasized the cosmocentric dimension of magico-religious realities, Durkheim and the supporters of a symbolic reading of religion underlined its anthropocentric aspect: the statements that it produces bear less upon the system of the world than upon the relationship between humans, they signify and express a certain state of a moral community rather than providing a conceptual framework to magical actions that aim to insure control over things. The object of an embryonic enterprise of rational explanation for the intellectualists, Nature becomes for the Durkheimians a backdrop animated by the ever-changing mental categories that human collectivities project upon it. Like religion, nature for the non-moderns is society transfigured; in the representations that a society has of nature, one can read the values, norms, codes through which humans think and organize their social life. And if these representations of the physical world still function in a reflective mode, it is no longer as a fantastical image of practices and phenomena reputed to be objective, but as a supposedly faithful indication of certain conditions of human existence which give to the symbolism of nature an undeniable power of conviction.

The Mystery of the Moderns

Positing cultures as so many symbolic devices which encode a uniform nature leads, as we just saw, to a great divide between those whose "vision of the world" reflects in a distorted way certain properties of reality, and those who claim to have a true apprehension of it thanks to scientific investigation. Yet relegating the non-Moderns to the obscurity of ideology and belief poses the additional inconvenience of making much more arduous the task of understanding the one culture that prides itself on having escaped relativism by basing its claims to universality on its capacity to delineate a natural order and discover its laws. The exaltation of Science as the archetype of valid knowledge and the transcendent source of truth inhibits any reflexive thought on this bizarre cosmology that the Moderns have created, since the very principle of its configuration—namely, the dissociation between an homogenous nature whose mysteries we have the means of penetrating and heterogeneous cultures prone to arbitrariness—cannot be questioned without threatening the equilibrium of this majestic modern edifice and undermining the preeminence that it assumes over the collection of disparate huts upon the rubbles of which it was constructed.

One could say that this is a well-known tune, given that for almost two centuries a chorus of lamentations has been deploring the disenchantment of the world brought on by science and technology; that reactionaries of all kinds, weak-kneed communitarians and those who long for the return to authenticity have sufficiently repeated this refrain for it to be necessary to take up again here. My purpose is not to denounce scientific or technical activity—a futile task—but rather to emphasize how difficult it is to grasp this central dimension of our own society with the kind of "view from afar" through which ethnologists observe and analyze non-modern societies, this productive tension between an initial situation of maximal distance and the means through which this distance is reduced. This gap is more difficult to maintain when observer and observed share the same received ideas and premises, even if their social origins, practical competences, and lifestyles may differ completely. In spite of the admirable critical gaze that Moderns have turned upon themselves before exploiting it in the study of the Other, despite an aptitude for amazement which, since Plato, has been the hallmark of the philosopher, it is difficult to stare with open eyes at a collection of individuals whose basic certainties we share. In fact, the analyst of modern societies, immersed like those he studies in a naturalist cosmology presumed to be coextensive with all of humanity, does not have the boost of a decentered point of view from where he could turn back upon himself, making him a stranger to himself, and invite him to question more vigorously the foundations of his own position in the world.

Of course, these considerations do not seek in any way to question the relevance of sociological studies of modern societies. They simply aim to clarify the reasons why ethnologists who have an experience of non-modern societies find themselves in a situation more favorable to overcoming their own myopia, because they are confronted by systems of objectification of the world which do not coincide with their own and which shed a different light on the latter, thus making its oddities and characteristic traits stand out. It is also not surprising that anthropologists such as Gregory Bateson or Roy Wagner were among the first to question the universality of the distribution of humans and of non-humans into separate essential systems, alongside specialists of other areas of knowledge—geographers, philosophers, or historians—whose familiarity with civilizations anterior or exterior to Western modernity had led to the same doubts.

It is also fair to recall that it is by exploring the very heart of the machinery producing modernity that a new branch of the tree of knowledge has arrived at the same result. The social studies of science (to which I was initiated by the work of Bruno Latour, particularly *Science in Action*) no longer uphold the pedagogical and normative discourse of classical epistemology, intended to purge Science of all social contaminations. On the contrary, they are interested in the daily life of scientific laboratories and in the development of controversies between researchers, in the production of facts and in the mechanisms of their ontological purification, in the discovery and experimentation of techniques, in industrial and political choices, in short, in the entanglement of theories and objects, of personal intentions and collective pressures. Far from bringing into question the validity of the laws of matter and life, as it has been accused of, this minutely detailed work of observing science in action renders the latter more complex and realistic, in any case less in accordance with the separation between the natural order and the social order upon which the Moderns have thought to found the originality of their cosmology. In restoring to humans and non-humans a common fate in the halls of academia, science studies wrest from positivism one of its most solid buttresses and, as an indirect consequence, offers to non-moderns the possibility of making their voice more audible and less deformed by the interference of the great dualist machineries.

Monisms and Symmetries

While for the past twenty years a growing number of scholars has started to draw the consequences of the exhaustion of dualism, these scholars are nevertheless far from agreeing on the path which could lead to another approach. The path most commonly taken can be qualified as phenomenological in the broad sense of the term. It favors describing the interlacing of the experience of the social and physical worlds while remaining as free as possible from the objectivist filters that hinder its immediate apprehension as a familiar environment. This approach thus challenges the quest for transcendent principles of a sociological, cognitive or ontological nature which would reduce phenomenal interactions to a purely expressive status, as well as the use of cultural categories that are too particularized or too historicized – society, value, thing-in-itself, or representation – to give an adequate account of the fluidity of the relationships conjoining humans and non-humans in a web of reciprocal identification. Because it attempts to come as close as possible to the manner in which the collectivities described live and perceive their engagement in the world, such an approach unquestionably gains in fidelity, or in credibility, in comparison with modes of knowing which emphasize the unveiling of structural or causal determinations. Yet one has to admit that the advantage of a more realistic account of local complexity is acquired at the expense of a lesser intelligibility of global complexity, that is to say of the multiple forms of relationships between beings. The effect of transparency obtained at the ethnographic scale becomes a factor of opacity as soon as one seeks to explain the reasons for the diversity of instituted points of view witnessed by ethnography and history. This is what we must now consider.

One branch of this phenomenological anthropology explicitly claims to adhere to a being-in-the-world ontology, drawing its inspiration from the Husserlian idea of *Umwelt* as the original basis of our experience and the horizon of our intentionality, as well as from the developments and reformulations of this idea by Heidegger and Merleau-Ponty. To this strictly philosophical base is added a shared interest in the pioneering work of Jacob von Uexkül on the subjective construction of the environment by animals and humans, and also in the more recent work of James Gibson on the notion of affordance in animal perception as a connecting device between certain salient properties of the apprehended object and certain behavioral orientations of the perceptive subject. It is by drawing on this heritage that Tim Ingold, for example, in "Hunting and Gathering as Ways of Perceiving the Environment," characterizes the relations of hunter-gatherers with their environment as a total immersion, an active, perceptive and practical engagement with the components of the lived world, by contrast with the classical anthropological perspective which begins by positing the exteriority of nature, which must then be grasped through thought and appropriated by symbols according to a determined cultural scheme before any practical activity might be carried out within it. Particularly developed among hunter-gatherers, this "ontology of dwelling" is however not their prerogative. According to Ingold, it expresses the human condition with more accuracy than its alternative, the Western ontology and its founding postulate of a mind detached from the world. The ontology of hunter-gatherers is true, adequate to reality, a faithful account of the complexity of the experience of beings, in contrast to the laborious constructions of Moderns, trapped in the analytics of dualism and the multiplicity of mediations between subject and object.

While such a position is entirely legitimate as a philosophical profession of faith, it is hardly so on the anthropological plane which Ingold aims to occupy. It simply inverses the common ethnocentric prejudice: it is no longer the animism of archaic peoples that appears as an incomplete version or a clumsy prefiguration of the true objectification of reality as Moderns establish it, but it is rather this very objectification that appears as a monstrous outgrowth dissimulating the truth of the primordial experience of the world, of which the hunter-gatherers, assisted by phenomenology, give us a better account. Yet, for anthropology, no ontology is better or more truthful in itself than another. Each of them must be examined not in terms of its plausibility or its moral virtues, of whether or not it authorizes a more authentic life or a more complete unveiling of its mechanisms, but for the variations that it manifests in regard to all the others in its manner of formatting our common experience of the world.

To decree the preeminence of a particular ontology on the pretext that it corresponds to the general lines of a philosophy whose seductive appeal is hard to

resist, is to hamper the understanding of the diversity of
forms of relationship with the world as surely as to
adopt contemporary Western codes and institutions as
a standard for ethnographic judgment. Ingold admits
this frankly: "nor am I concerned to set up a comparison between the 'intentional worlds' of hunter-gatherers and Western scientists or humanists," and adds, "it
is of course an illusion to suppose that such a comparison could be made on level terms." There is, however,
nothing illusory in such a project, short of presuming
that Pygmies and astrophysicists are different in nature,
that their respective means of perceiving and experienc-
ing the continuities and discontinuities of the world
answer to mechanisms that are so heterogeneous as to
locate them in parallel and incommunicable planes of
reality. Nothing however prevents a young seal hunter
of the Siberian Tchoukotka from becoming a respected
geographer, as was the case of Nicholas Daurkin, who
drew the first maps of the region for Catherine II
during the eighteenth century; nor a poacher of the
Sologne such as Raboliot from moving among the
"intentional world" of hunter-gatherers, at least if we
give credence to the talent of novelist Maurice
Genevoix. It is not their faculties that distinguish the
hunter-gatherers from academics, but the schemes of
coding and parceling out phenomenal reality by means
of which they have learned to couch and transmit their
experience of things, schemes issuing from historical
choices that privileged, at a given time and place,
certain sets of relations to humans and non-humans, in
such a way as to allow for the combination of these
relationships into *sui generis* ensembles—already constituted before the birth of the individuals that actualize
them—to be experienced as naturally coherent. In his

iconoclastic ambition to eliminate all the social mediations that supposedly obscure the powerful self-
evidence of practical activity—linguistic categories,
norms of behavior, values, systems of education and
knowledge—Ingold seems to forget that we can only
access the other, and thus their experience of the world,
through these devices of translation, insofar as they
shape the account that each human can give of this
experience. The task of the anthropologist is not to
assess the truth of ontologies; it is rather to understand
how, starting from a position of practical engagement
that one can suppose to be common to humanity, all of
these ontologies, including our own, are or have been
considered self-evident to some people in certain places
and in certain epochs.

The striving of phenomenological anthropology to suspend itself between beings and Being makes
it sensitive to the slightest breeze which pushes it alter-
nately toward a fluid world from which humans are
almost eclipsed or toward an overflow of meaning
imposed by them. Thus, and although he also situates
himself within a relational ontology and an ethic of
dwelling, Augustin Berque (in *Être humains sur la
terre*), remains at the threshold of this generalized
subjectification of beings and things through practical
interaction Ingold's work illustrates. In his attempt to
formulate an ethics of the ecumene, that is to say of the
earth as the dwelling of humanity—an expression of the
Heideggerian idea of "worldhood (*Weltlichkeit*)," the
source of a relation of truth transcendent to singular
existences—Berque first attends to the demands of
temporal context. Analyzing what he calls the "trajectivity" of an environment or of an epoch requires on the
part of the observer an "effort of objectification" all the

more stringent given that this observer is immersed in the "epochality" of the world where he lives. Far from validating the perspective of hunter-gatherers, phenomenology should thus simultaneously go beyond both modern thought and the holistic thought of archaic peoples. But Berque sets himself apart from Ingold above all by an unambiguous, *a priori* sociocentricity: "it is the projection of human values upon the environment that makes it a human place." The critical approach of Ingold is animated, on the contrary, by the rebuttal of such a projective process, a surreptitious means, according to him, of perpetuating the very distinction between a mute nature and a ventriloquist culture that the phenomenological approach proposes to abolish. Between the effacement of humans in the virginity of a practical world without rules or representations and the preponderance of the human in the definition of that which makes sense on the earth, the middle path of being-in-the-world thus lurches through numerous zigzags.

Another means of adopting a middling position consists of giving equivalent weight to the two poles of nature and culture by examining how scientific and technical practice operates a kind of triage and recomposition in the hybrids that it produces in order to better distribute them between the "pure forms" of subject and object, society and the physical world, the universal and the relative. This is the approach that sociologists gathered around Michel Callon and Bruno Latour have adopted with the goal of building a symmetrical anthropology. Fueled by the ambition of breathing new life into the study of sciences and techniques, they worked to go beyond the first principle of symmetry formulated by David Bloor. Bloor recommended that one give equal treatment to truth and error, the successes of science as much as its failures, in contrast to the conventional epistemology and sociology of knowledge which are interested more in the mishaps of scientific production and in the obstacles that it has to surmount than in its normal activity when it is recognized and institutionalized. Yet, this first step remains itself asymmetrical because it explains the success of truth and the failure of falsehood through the ideological and social constraints affecting scientific practice. Consequently it envisions nature as an intellectual construction, an object the configuration of which varies according to historic circumstances and locally dominant modes of thought, granting to society the sole privilege of defining what is or is not legitimate science, hence endowing the former with a robust realism that Durkheim would not have rebuked. A more balanced symmetry is thus required to reveal the mechanisms which, in laboratories, research offices or industrial sites produce inextricable mixtures of physical phenomena and measuring instruments, of economic requirements and of material apparatuses, of judicial laws and principles of method. It is necessary, in sum, to pursue the incessant work of mediation between quasi-objects and quasi-subjects everywhere it operates in the modern world without stopping at the official version that mediators give of what they do.

Such an enterprise is inspired by ethnography: just as anthropologists who describe non-modern societies link in the same ensemble hunting rituals, ancestor cults, land tenure and forms of authority, so too do sociologists promoting a symmetrical approach labor to find, behind the dualist discourses of the Moderns, the means by which they create ontological mixtures, the processes which determine the properties of humans and non-humans and define their relationships, their forms of grouping and their respective competences. However, unlike societies bound to a territory that ethnologists have for a long time exclusively dealt with, the objects of the new sociology of sciences are freed from local moorings. They are deployed in networks of common practice seeking to create, by reciprocal translation, hybrid combinations of nature and culture, so that scientists and the phenomena they objectify, engineers and their machines, administrators and their rules, are unveiled for what they are, each a spokesperson for every other node in the network.

This anthropology also aims to be symmetrical in another way. Challenging the Great Divide, it locates Moderns and non-Moderns on the same plane and proposes to consider identically all the collectives within which the repartitions between beings and properties are at work: as much those of whom anthropology has made a specialty, those producers of ontologies and cosmologies that Moderns study without adhering to them, as the collectives wherein is elaborated the positive knowledge to which we adhere without truly studying the concrete manner by which it is produced. In denying to modern dualism the structuring function that it had hitherto been granted, in emphasizing that, everywhere and always, humans enlist crowds of non-humans in the fabric of communal life, symmetrical anthropology places on an equal footing Amazonian tribes and biological laboratories, pilgrimages to Our Lady and synchrotrons. Here is indeed a program that should not leave ethnologists indifferent, bearer as it is of the much awaited reconciliation between the exotic and the familiar, between scholarly exegeses sparked by the non-moderns and the opaque banality that occludes the most complex devices of the production of modernity.

But how is one to operate a triage between all these stabilized mediations? How is one to compare these collectives so diverse by the resources they mobilize? How is one to account for the differential gaps which distinguish them? Symmetrical anthropology brings to this conundrum only a partial answer, in large part conditioned by the particular nature of its objects of study. The Moderns and those who are not would be distinguished essentially by the fact that the former have created large networks which can accommodate a quantity of non-humans, notably machines, thus making the community resulting from this mixture more intimate and more complex (as Latour shows, in *We Have Never Been Modern*). The contrast is thus quantitative rather than qualitative. It resides in the extension of networks and the density of their interconnections rather than in heterogeneous forms of combination between nature and society. In fact, symmetrical anthropology still lacks a general theory of the stabilization of human and non-human collectives into particular forms of practices. But to constitute such a theory would no doubt entail going against certain principles of actor-network theory upon which symmetrical anthropology is founded; it would require giving more credit to the instituted devices that organize the manner by which hybrids are produced, and which make certain configurations of humans and non-humans possible or impossible. One would also need to admit that every distribution demands a collection of filters whose mesh size must be fitted to the material to be sorted; that to compare is, in short, to capture the diversity of structures by means of which humans themselves effect the triage and the recomposition of reality. It is true that Latour is not oblivious to this point when he defines *anthropos* as "a changer or blender of morphisms" (in *Nous n'avons jamais été modernes*, in my translation). The character of humans is indeed to be great distributors of ontological destinies, skilled in presenting themselves under different masks according to the forms that they adopt to delegate themselves in part to animals, machines or divinities. Yet these forms are neither random nor contingent. They are not born from the whim of *ad hoc* negotiations nor do they extinguish themselves at the periphery of networks; they outline a combinatory upon which humanity has at all times had to draw in order to give order and meaning to the relations that it weaves with the world and with itself.

An attempt to eliminate the duality of the subject and of the world when describing collective life should not lead to neglecting research on the framing structures that account for the coherence and the regularity in the behavior of members of a community, in the distinctive style of their public and private actions as well as in the codified accounts they give of them. This tension between the constraint of forms and the original truth of experience is certainly not new; it lies at the heart of the modern development of the philosophy of knowledge. It has recently taken a singular vigor through the debates which animate the cognitive sciences. On one side, we find the partisans of embodied or situated cognition, the disciples of Gibson and all those who challenge the dualism of mind and body in order to emphasize the structuring of understanding as an emergent property stemming from the interactions between the organism and its environment; on the other, the neo-Chomskyians, who defend a modular theory of the mind conceived as an assemblage of specialized devices for the treatment of information. In granting an immoderate privilege to individual experience, the first group fails to explain the stabilization of shared representations and the role they play in the structuring of practices; in universalizing *a priori* categories of thought, the second group falls short of accounting for the diversity of its expressions according to contexts. To speak like the linguists, a too exclusive attention to the point of view of performance masks the organization of competence, while the search for cognitive conditions of competence leads to the neglect of its expression in performance. In both cases, the comprehension of the diversity of systems of relationship to the world is jeopardized.

Revisiting the question of the institution and stabilization of collective forms of experience thus becomes a matter of urgency. One might think that such an enterprise is outdated, so much has the study of facts of structure been neglected by the social sciences for the past twenty years. In reaction to a structuralism that is more caricatured than really understood—most often reduced to an abstract formalism, which would actually be hard to find in the works of Lévi-Strauss, Benveniste, or Dumézil—the entire arsenal of spontaneity, of creativity, and of sentiment has been mobilized; the causal agency of social actors has been celebrated; the importance of resistance to hegemony and oppression in historical dynamics has been underlined. This current tendency to restore a praxis that would be self-evident at last since it has been liberated from its alienations—how we wish this were actually true!—is directed against adversaries fabricated for the circumstance whose sacramental denunciation passes for a theoretical proposition—it is the fault of Kant, the fault of Descartes, the fault of Lévi-Strauss. However, the driving force of conscious agency is hardly supported by ethnological and sociological data; monograph after monograph, they show us that the customs and behavior observable in a collective do not proceed from deliberate agreement but display a consistency and a degree of automatism which its members are generally unable to relate back to a cultural model or a system of explicit rules. From whence do these shared attitudes vis-à-vis humans and non-humans come? They are so engrained that they seem to manifest a program, yet they are so profoundly interiorized that they almost never surface in a reflexive manner. What produces their permanence and generality? Imitation, some say. Certainly, but why then do we find analogous dispositions in regions of the world so distant from each other that any kind of diffusion may be excluded? Reproducing what one witnesses, adjusting to or emulating the conduct of others may explain the diffusion within a community of practice of a kind of behavior or a type of utterance, not why these emerged in the first place, the modalities under which they are expressed nor the fact that they are compatible with other genres of behavior and utterance within the same community. In order to account for such automatisms we can invoke neither the repertoires of rules instilled through education, nor the public deliberations in regard to the best choices possible. We should rather see in these convergences of judgments and actions the effect of cognitive and sensory-motor templates orienting the expression of distinctive behaviors, schemes of practice that, in order to be effective, must remain implicit and shielded from collective speculation.

Universalism and Relativism

The search for regularities and the construction of invariants are thus back on the agenda again. But how is one to combine an enterprise of this nature, marked by the seal of scientific universalism, with the relative character of the conceptual device by means of which we express our own objectification of the world? How can a demand for anthropological intelligibility applicable to all humans keep pace with the statement that the tools we employ in this task are the contingent product of the historical trajectory of a single civilization? A first step consists precisely in ridding ourselves of the sterile and paralyzing opposition between universalism and relativism. These two notions are, in fact, mechanisms of epistemological decantation that transcribe the opposition of nature and culture into incompatible credos: to matter and life, universal laws; to institutions, relative norms. Between the two there is however a small measure of leeway allowing some people to reduce the scope of the relative by invoking the effects of determinations working everyway in the same manner, and other people to cast doubt on the purity of procedures and intentions mobilized in the production of scientific truths. To those who remain unsatisfied with such a situation, it is common to reproach a blindness to the stubborn evidence of facts and a propensity to yield to irrationality or moral skepticism. Must I then specify that I in no way challenge the reality of Earth's attraction or photosynthesis, no more than I contest the great heterogeneity of the solutions that humanity has found for the treatment of the dead or the socialization of children? It is evidently not the legitimacy of scientific work that I am questioning here, nor the validity of the explanations that it produces, but rather the conventional epistemological framework that many of its practitioners adopt spontaneously, as well as its pretention to serve as the standard for judging what appears to differ from it.

It seems increasingly obvious that the reification of properties attributed to nature and culture found in research programs, gnoseologies, and heterogeneous systems of values can only lead to an impasse in the enterprise that commands my attention, understanding the diversity of relationships that humans establish between themselves and with non-humans. On this subject, it is imperative to suspend all judgment on the truth values of a given practice or discourse if we do not wish to eternally measure our understanding of beings and things against the yardstick of a transcendent prototype. I am willing to believe, for example, that a gene therapy has more chance of success than a shamanic cure, but to define the former as anchored in positive reality and the latter in the symbolic and the imaginary does not do justice to the freedom of spirit of scientific thought. The respective properties of these two healing practices, the combinations and mediations that they operate, the interactions they create, the ontological divisions they reflect and the circumstances of their coming into existence all become incommensurable when shamanism becomes a derived object of inquiry, apprehended according to the greater or lesser gap that it is supposed to evidence in regard to the criteria of biological truth and therapeutic efficacy of modern medicine. To say this does not amount to a relativist profession of faith, relativism being possible only when buttressed, more or less openly, by a natural universal order serving as a backdrop from which an infinity of particular cultural formulas emerge with vividness. Abolish this canvas, without denying the existence of that portion of reality which it has the mission of representing, and the elements of the *proscenium* recompose themselves in a completely new landscape; a landscape where nature and society, humans and non-humans, individuals and collectives no longer appear to us as distributed among substances, processes and representations, but as instituted expressions of relations between multiple entities whose ontological status and capacity of action vary according to the positions they occupy in relationship to others.

The stabilization in frameworks of thought and action of our practical engagement with the world—what one might call "worlding"—is based primarily upon our capacity to detect qualities in existing things and to consequently infer the links that they are susceptible to maintain and the actions of which they are capable. It thus hardly makes sense to oppose, as modernist epistemology does, a single and true world, composed of all the objects and phenomena potentially knowable, to the multiple and relative worlds that each one of us creates through our daily subjective experience. It is more plausible to admit that that which exists outside of our body and in interface with it presents itself as a finite ensemble of qualities and relations which can or cannot be actualized by humans according to the circumstances and to the ontological options which guide them, rather than as a complete and autonomous totality awaiting to be represented and explained according to diverse points of view. Neither Platonic prototypes ready to be captured more or less completely by our faculties, nor pure social constructions that would give meaning and form to a raw material, the objects of our environment, material and immaterial, amount to packets of qualities of which certain are detected, others ignored. This is one of the important lessons to be drawn from Lévi-Strauss in *La Pensée Sauvage* (1962). The variety in forms of worlding, and the guarantee that this process can be studied scientifically, therefore derives from the fact that the differential actualization of qualities and relationships does not occur at random, but is guided by elementary inferences in regard to the assignment of qualities to objects—humans as well as non-humans, real as well as imaginary—and in regard to the types of links which unite these qualities. A modest empiricism based upon this type of principle suffices to ensure the possibility of anthropological work, namely describing and systematizing in the most culturally neutral way as possible the different manners in which specific organisms inhabit the world, identify in it this or that property for their use and contribute to its transformation by weaving with it, and between them, constant or occasional ties of a very diverse but not unlimited nature.

Conclusion

One does not have to be a great seer to predict that the relationship between humans and nature will, in all probability, be the most important question of the present century. It suffices to look around oneself to be convinced of this: climate change, the erosion of biodiversity, the multiplication of transgenic organisms, the exhaustion of fossil fuels, the pollution of fragile environments and of large urban centers, the accelerating disappearance of tropical forests, all have become an issue of public debate at the global scale and fuel the disquiet of numerous inhabitants of our planet. At the same time, it has become increasingly difficult to continue to believe that nature is a completely separate domain from social life, hypostatized according to circumstances under the species of a nourishing mother, of a spiteful stepmother, or of a mysterious beauty to be unveiled; a domain that humans attempt to understand and control and whose whims they occasionally suffer, but which constitutes a field of autonomous regularities within which values, conventions, and ideologies have no place. This fantasy is now vanishing: where does nature stop and culture begin in regard to global warming, in the thinning of the ozone layer, in the production of specialized cells from stem cells? Clearly the question no longer makes any sense. Above all, beyond the many ethical issues it raises, this new state of things upsets older conceptions of the human person and its components, as well as of the constitution of individual and collective identity; at least in the Western world where, in contrast to what happens elsewhere, we have been used to distinguishing fairly clearly the natural and the artificial in humans and their environment. In other places, in China or Japan, for example, where the idea of nature is unknown and where the human body is not conceived as a sign of the soul and the replica of a transcendent model—a divine creation formerly, a genotype today—this kind of problem does not arise.

Thus it is above all in Europe and North America that the development of biotechnologies causes unease attesting to the discomfort provoked by the profound questioning of beliefs and norms which used to organize relations with nature. Elsewhere, it is rather the changes in climate and the environment which threaten life habits and ways of thinking. Yet, whether they are legitimate or whether they are fantastical, these fears are rarely allayed by scientific explanations; first because these explanations are not accessible to everybody, but above all because the attitudes of the denizens of the world in regard to these questions are rooted in diverse cultural substrata, the formation and development of which are relatively autonomous in comparison with scientific developments, even in the great industrialized nations. It is this kind of substratum that anthropology has begun to study, not as a response to "social demands" (e.g., the acceptability of certain biological techniques, of certain ways of combating the greenhouse effect...), but rather because it has become indispensable in the West to reflect upon the effects of the disintegration of our notion of the natural world by locating this problem in a more general framework; this framework would allow the examination of the different conceptions of the biological dimension of humans and of the relations with the physical environment that they have developed in various places in the course of history.

Although it boasts solid antecedents, such an enterprise has hitherto remained merely sketched, primarily because of disciplinary compartmentalization and the specialization of fields of expertise. The remarkable works of historians retracing the evolution of sensibilities toward plants and animals, or describing the modification of climates and landscapes, have thus been essentially focused on the Western world and its colonial projections. Because of the nature of their object, philosophy and epistemology have also focused exclusively on European thought when attempting to understand the successive mutations of the idea of nature and the scientific discoveries that these changes allowed. It is still solely the contemporary West and its economic and political convulsions that are dealt with by a number of excellent sociological studies of the ideology and the practices of conservation movements, of the contrasting perceptions of the environment by rural peoples and city dwellers, or of the subjective appreciation of ecological and biotechnological risks. By contrast, human geography has turned its gaze and its methods toward other latitudes and has produced fine-grained analyses of the effects of natural conditions on human activities. Monographs devoted to the relations of societies with their environment in the inter-tropical belt have multiplied in the course of the last decades, bringing a rich crop of data on the means by which societies fashion their environment according to local physical constraints. Nevertheless, because of the scale of analysis adopted in these studies, they have often neglected the advice of the noted tropical geographer Pierre Gourou not to study solely the ecological setting, but also how humans think about it. This is why one turns more readily to anthropology when looking for detailed information on folk-knowledge, systems of classification, beliefs and the techniques by which interactions between societies and their environments are mediated in a great variety of regions of the globe.

Anthropology, understood as a general knowledge of social life through the diversity of its cultural expressions, finds itself in a particularly favorable position for attempting to tie the threads of these diverse approaches. Firstly because it has in some ways inherited the philosophical problematic of the relationship between nature and culture when, in the second half of the nineteenth century, it took on the mission of understanding and explaining increasingly abundant information regarding the strange way by which peoples who had fallen into the sphere of European colonialism conceived of their links to plants and animals, treating certain species as kin, attributing to others an ancestral or divine status. Hence the origin of the great debates concerning animism, or "primitive totemism," in which the founders of the discipline sought to account for the cognitive or social origin of those intellectual constructions that, in neglecting the distinctions between humans and non-humans, seemed to stand against the claims of reason. But the anthropologist's interest in the question of the interface between the biological, the cultural, and the social goes well beyond the fortuitous circumstances of its genesis, because all the empirical objects that anthropologists study on the other side of the world or closer to home—systems of kinship, marriage and descent, conceptions of personhood and of the body, environmental knowledge and practices, the management of physical and moral sufferings—lie precisely at the juncture of biological and cognitive data, at the interface between the properties of physical objects and the schemes—individual as well as collective—through which these properties are expressed and transformed.

In order for anthropology to fulfill this mission, however, it must forswear the *pas de deux* between nature naturing and nature natured of which the preceding pages have traced a few figures. Granted, nature is only accessible to us through the devices of cultural coding which objectify it: esthetic forms, scientific paradigms, technical mediations, systems of classification, religious beliefs. Granted, natural phenomena can only be apprehended as translated by a kaleidoscope of practices and representations which underline, isolate, or overshadow certain physical properties, certain types of action upon matter, certain relationships of analogy or contrast. The study of uses and representations of the body and of the environment should thus not be an end in itself, but rather a privileged means of accessing the intelligibility of the various structures which organize relations between humans and with non-humans. But the mistrust that anthropologists feel toward theories which postulate a direct relationship of determination between the genome or the ecosystem and social institutions should not make them more receptive to approaches that envision culture as an entirely specific order of realities. The former draw erroneous conclusions from the evolutionary continuity of organisms, because they neglect the uniquely social processes of differentiation deriving from the diversity of modes of human life, while the latter choose to ignore this continuity by only considering the symbolic dimensions of social life; this has the effect of rendering it eternally mysterious and difficult to compare in its different instantiations. It is time for anthropology to abandon this futile quest for prime movers and tune into the sciences which share the same endeavor: producing knowledge about the nature of being human. The research of neurobiologists on the mechanisms of perception; of developmental psychologists on the formation of ontological categories; of primatologists and prehistorians on the schemes of technical action; or of biogeographers on the evolution of biocenoses, offer many precious lessons on the modes of apprehending and interacting with non-humans.

In short, the critique of the opposition between nature and culture with which I have engaged implicates a vast reworking of the conceptual tools employed for dealing with the relationships between natural objects and social beings. It is not sufficient to show that this opposition does not exist for numerous non-modern societies, or that it appears late in the development of Western thought. It is necessary to integrate it in a new analytical field within which modern naturalism, far from constituting the standard by which to judge cultures distant in time or space, would only be one of the possible expressions of more general schemes governing the objectification of the world and others. Confronted with the existence of a multitude of "associated bodies," to borrow Merleau-Ponty's formula, humans have strived to organize the relations they maintain with these entities according to social formulas of which there is probably a limited number. This involves first choices about the siting of ontological boundaries, and thus the structure of cosmologies: continuities between humans and non-humans treated according to a regime of identical sociability; transfer by analogy of properties of natural objects to social taxonomies; correspondence or action at a distance between elements of the macrocosm and elements of the microcosm; separation between the sphere of humans and the rest of the world, etc. Second, it involves the systems of value which orient the practical relations with the Others, human and non-human, and which, when they locally have a dominant position, confer to a society its distinctive style: the expectations of reciprocity, predatory appropriation, the disinterested gift, protection, production, etc. Finally, it involves the devices of classification by means of which the elements of the world are distributed into more or less extensive nomenclatures. One can surmise that all of the schemes available to humanity for defining relationships with the components of the world exist under the form of mental structures, partly innate, partly stemming from the properties of social life. But these structures are not all compatible with each other, so that every cultural system, and each type of social organization, is the product of a triage and a combination which, although contingent, is often repeated in history with comparable results. To specify the nature of these elements, to elucidate their rules of composition and to draw up a typology of their arrangements is the task that anthropology should set itself as a priority. ■

List of works referenced

Ardener, E. "Belief and the Problem of Women," in J. S. La Fontaine (ed.), *The Interpretation of Ritual: Essays in Honour of A. I. Richards*, pp. 135-138. London: Tavistock, 1972.

Ardener, E. "The 'Problem' Revisited", in S. Ardener (ed.), *Perceiving Women*, pp. 19-27. London: Malaby Press, 1975.

Atran, S. *Cognitive foundations of natural history: Towards an anthropology of science*. Cambridge / Paris: Cambridge University Press / Editions de la Maison des Sciences de l'Homme, 1990.

Bateson, G. *Steps to an Ecology of Mind*. New York: Ballantine Books, 1972.

Berlin, B. *Ethnobiological Classification: Principles of Categorization of Plants and Animals in Traditional Societies*. Princeton: Princeton University Press, 1992.

Berque, A. *Médiance: De milieux en paysages*. Montpellier: RECLUS, 1990.

Berque, A. *Être humains sur la terre: Principes d'éthique de l'écoumène*. Paris: Le débat-Gallimard, 1996.

Bloor, D. *Knowledge and Social Imagery*. Chicago: The University of Chicago Press, 1976.

Dawkins, R. *The Selfish Gene*. Oxford & New York: Oxford University Press, 1976.

Descola, P. "Societies of nature and the nature of society," in A. Kuper (ed.), *Conceptualizing Society*, pp. 107-126. London and New York: Routledge, 1992.

Descola, P. *In the Society of Nature: A Native Ecology in Amazonia* (N. Scott, Trans.). Cambridge: Cambridge University Press, 1994.

Descola, P. *Par-delà nature et culture*. Paris: Gallimard, 2005. (English translation, *Beyond Nature and Culture*, Chicago: The University of Chicago Press, in press).

Douglas, M. *Implicit Meanings: Essays in anthropology*. London: Routledge & Kegan Paul, 1975.

Durkheim, E. *Les formes élémentaires de la vie religieuse: Le système totémique en Australie*. Paris: Presses Universitaires de France, 1960 [1912].

Evans-Pritchard, E., E. "The intellectualist (English) interpretation of magic." *Bulletin of the Faculty of Arts* 1, pp 282-311. Cairo University, 1933.

Foucault, M. *The Order of Things: An Archaeology of the Human Sciences*. New York: Pantheon Books, 1971 [1966].

Frazer, J. G. *The Golden Bough: A Study in Magic and Religion*. Abridged edition. London: MacMillan, 1922.

French, D. "The Relationship of Anthropology to Studies in Perception and Cognition," in S. Koch (ed.), *Psychology: A study of a science*. Volume 6, pp. 388-428. New York: McGraw-Hill, 1963.

Geertz, C. "The Wet and the Dry: Traditional Irrigation in Bali and Morocco." *Human Ecology* 1 (1), 1972.

Gibson, J. J. *The Ecological Approach to Visual Perception*. Boston: Houghton Mifflin, 1979.

Godelier, M. *The Mental and the Material: Thought, Economy and Society* (M. Thom, trans.). London: Verso, 1996 [1984].

Harris, M. *Cows, Pigs, Wars and Witches: The Riddles of Culture*. New York: Random House, 1974.

Harris, M. "Lévi-Strauss et la palourde: Réponse à la Conférence Gildersleeve de 1972." *L'Homme* XVI (2-3): pp. 5-22, 1976.

Ingold, T. "Hunting and gathering as Ways of Perceiving the Environment," in R. Ellen & K. Fukui (eds.), *Redefining Nature: Ecology, Culture and Domestication*, pp. 117-155. Oxford: Berg, 1996.

Jakobson, R., & L. R. Waugh. *The Sound Shape of Language*. Bloomington: Indiana University Press, 1979.

Latour, B. *Science in Action: How to Follow Scientists and Engineers Through Society*. Cambridge: Harvard University Press, 1987.

Latour, B. *We Have Never Been Modern*. Cambridge: Harvard University Press, 1994.

Lévi-Strauss, C. "Structuralism and Ecology. The Gildersleeve Lecture." *Information sur les sciences sociales/ Social Science Information*, Vol. 12 (1): 7-23, 1972.

Lévi-Strauss, C. "Structuralisme et empirisme." *L'Homme* XVI (2-3): 23-38, 1976.

Lévi-Strauss, C. *Le regard éloigné*. Paris: Plon, 1983.

Malinowski, B. *A Scientific Theory of Culture and Other Essays*. Oxford & New York: Oxford University Press, 1960 [1944].

Marx, K. *Selected Writings*, edited by Lawrence H. Simon. Indianapolis & Cambridge: Hackett Publishing Company, 1994.

Pouillon, J. "Remarques sur le verbe 'croire'," in M. Izard & P. Smith (eds.), *La fonction symbolique: essais d'anthropologie*, Paris: Gallimard, 1979.

Pouillon, J. *Le cru et le su*. Paris: Le Seuil, 1993.

Rappaport, R. A. *Ecology, Meaning, and Religion*. Berkeley: North Atlantic Books, 1979.

Rickert, H. *Science and History: A Critique of Positivist Epistemology* (G. Reisman, trans.). Princeton: Van Nostrand, 1962 [1899]

Ross, E. "Food Taboos, Diet and Hunting Strategy: the Adaptation to Animals in Amazon Cultural Ecology." *Current Anthropology* 19 (1): 1-36, 1978.

Sahlins, M. *Culture and Practical Reason*. Chicago & London: The University of Chicago Press, 1976.

Sahlins, M. *The Western Illusion of Human Nature: With Reflections on the Long History of Hierarchy, Equality and the Sublimation of Anarchy in the West, and Comparative Notes on Other Conceptions of the Human Condition*. Chicago: Prickly Paradigm Press, 2008.

Steward, J. H. *Handbook of South American Indians*, volumes 1-7. Washington: Smithsonian Institution, Bureau of American Ethnology, 1944-1949.

Steward, J. H. *Theory of Culture Change: The Methodology of Multilinear Evolution*. Urbana: University of Illinois Press, 1955.

Sturtevant, W. "Studies in Ethnoscience." *American Anthropologist* 66 (3): 99-131, 1964.

Wagner, R. *The Invention of Culture*. Chicago & London: The University of Chicago Press, 1981 [1975].

Also available from Prickly Paradigm Press:

continued